THE RESPONSIBLES

1817

HARPER & ROW, PUBLISHERS

New York   Evanston   San Francisco   London

. . . . .

THE RESPONSIBLES

William S. White

FIRST EDITION

STANDARD BOOK NUMBER: 06-014619-2

LIBRARY OF CONGRESS CATALOG CARD NUMBER: 79-95991

TO A LADY:

my sister, Doris White Rowe

CONTENTS

. . .

BOOK ONE

The Way They Are

• • •

In an age of a puerile and one-book cynicism among the campus and postcampus young and of a sour and obesely materialistic skepticism among the middle-aged and the elderly, a certain important truth yet abides. Notwithstanding all disillusionments and scandals and acts of peculation and of demagoguery, the United States of America is nevertheless sometimes served by a rare, tough breed of truly responsible politicians.

If only a lackwit would say that all is well with all our politics, the perceptive person could all the same take heart in what is after all the central reality. This is that taking men as they are and neither expecting perfection nor yet rejecting the attainably good in search of the impossibly ideal, we have in the best of our politicians the best of all possible political worlds.

The bad in the system and in its workings is all too evident; the good in it is far from inconsiderable and very far from generally known. This, then, is an exposition and a celebration of the Responsibles of American public life; of those, living or dead, who have given more than they have taken from the common human fund of the Great Republic. All have had warts, of course; all have made mistakes. But all, too, have offered in the end a sturdy vindication of the essential vitality, strength and decency of the American political experience. The salute here is not from Pollyanna, who is in any case long dead and gone, but it is genuine and earned. And it is doubly earned because responsible political action is, more often than not, not only denied reward in its own time but actually punished until the future and hindsight can come to the rescue of truth.

To begin at the beginning, the first quality of the Responsibles is courage, though usually a courage touched by the sweat of honest fear and by the temptation, at least, to wait until later to say or to do the thing that must be done. The Responsibles are authentic heroes; but, being sensible fellows, they do not rush to grasp the hero's role. They have no compulsion to glamorous suicide.

There is in them a great determination, though this, too, is not unmixed with the hope that some other man will stand on the barricade, some other George or Jack walk first across the minefield that may stand athwart the route march to duty and obligation.

There is in them a homely, a roundly mundane, quality of common sense exercised, at the last, with a central humility to be found, again at last, in every one of the Responsibles, vain or arrogant though he may be in some things and at some times.

4

And there is in them a matchless perception of what *must* be done and how it must be done and how it must *not* be done, a perception that lies at the heart of what is best in Anglo-American politics and is, indeed, in itself, the greatest gift to the world of the Anglo-American political heritage. This is a bone-deep, a blood-inherited, prerecognition of the true meaning and the ultimate purpose of politics. This is to make things *work;* but neither so well and so slickly as to deny the government's and the people's right to be wrong; nor yet so loosely, so poorly, as to goad the rational to throw out the whole works for another system that will assure that every train will run right on time.

This quality, this intuition, firstly of what is necessary, secondly of what is possible and thirdly of what is simply and finally tolerable to the nation, informs, pervades and arms the Responsibles. It is what makes them tick; it is what makes them possible. It is what makes them survive in a national political atmosphere in which intellectual hucksterism is all too acceptable.

What the Responsibles know and act upon is that while achievement and performance are the sole aims of political activity, this is not to say that any end is worth *any* means. Politics, if much more than a game, is still not to be seen as a blood battle. The objective is to win the end, of course, but the end is not to be won by the literal destruction of one's opposition. The opponent is to be pushed out of the way, even knocked soundly down, but then he is to be picked up, dusted off and left with such dignity as may be possible to him in all the circumstances. For in the great, continuing contest, today's antagonist may be tomorrow's desperately needed recruit for a new action.

This might be called the rule of essential civility. It is essential because a responsible politics is not and cannot be a Balkan politics, in which the adversary is killed in the literal sense and then, to make doubly sure, is carted lifelessly away to top some bonfire both celebrating a victory and satisfying a lust for revenge. For the abandonment of civility is not only unethical but also self-defeating—or, as it would be put in the patois of the present, counterproductive.

So it is that an acceptance of what is both the rule and the intractable reality of effective political action—that is, the practice of forgiveness after battle for reasons both human and practical—lies at the root of both the personality and the procedures of every Responsible. And it is here, upon what is actually the first step in the ladder of responsibility, that many an American politician has stumbled and fallen.

It is, for one illustration, as good as certain that Richard Nixon, always an able politician who only after trial and error became also a responsible one, would long before 1968 have become President had his earlier career not been marked by failure to apprehend the profound fact that the American ethos unconsciously requires of its leaders that they display a certain irreducible element of tolerance to their adversaries.

By 1960, indeed, Nixon had grasped this subtlety; in his campaign against John Kennedy he sought to act upon this new awareness. The "New Nixon," however, was at that time too new, in the sense that the voters had not fully understood the change in him. Even so, he lost only narrowly to Kennedy. The precise and singly over-mastering reason for that Democratic victory may be endlessly argued. Perhaps it was the contribution of strength in the South, and notably in Texas, by Lyndon Johnson as the Kennedy running mate. To cut it finer, there are those who believe that not Johnson but rather what happened during the campaign in a Dallas hotel to Johnson and to Mrs. Johnson was itself the wind of chance that turned a Presidential election, for the far-rightists who jeered and jostled a Southern lady may have reversed a clearly strong pro-Nixon trend in Texas. Though this episode may be considered less than deci-sive—and to this writer's knowledge Johnson saw the possible impact in a fraction of a second and was in no hurry to leave this scene of squalid bitterness until it had been well photographed and thus evidentially estab-lished for the future—the point is unchanged. John Kennedy himself once told me that he had viewed it as one of the crises of that campaign. "Old Lyndon," he said with a smile, "was sure not exactly loping out of that hotel lobby." At all events, the fact is that Nixon did come within a micromillimeter of defeating Kennedy; and whatever degree of importance may be given to the affair in Dallas the central truth is that one thing, and one alone, in Nixon's past denied to him the Presidency of the United States in 1960.

This was a public memory, vague as to details but widely held, that the old Nixon in power had been not simply a fighter in politics but, at times, a guerrilla fighter who lacked the indispensable instinct not to press

7

one's adversaries too hard, too long and too harshly, no matter how few these adversaries.

Richard Nixon, that is to say, was pursued overlong by (the dreadful word is unavoidable) an "image" that had long since lost its validity. If his conduct in the lost 1960 Presidential campaign had been responsible, his behavior in the successful 1968 campaign was highly so. This was especially and poignantly the case on the issue of the war in Vietnam. In this area, he never uttered a word that could have made more difficult the already difficult position of a sitting Democratic President, Lyndon Johnson, in finding some tolerable way out of the jungles of Vietnam.

There were two reasons for this sensitive and perceptive reticence. One was that Richard Nixon had now acquired the instinct for a certain partisan and ideological restraint that is so absolutely necessary in some areas of national political life. Another reason was that he realized actually far more acutely than did his opponent, Hubert Humphrey, that whatever the outcome of the looming November election, the winner, whatever his name, must not in the course of the struggle have already thrown away the power of the Presidency to choose among future options in dealing with the North Vietnamese Communists and the Vietcong. This was the central reality, as Nixon was fully aware, regardless of which course the President-to-be might at length decide to follow. Even if the ultimate decision was to forfeit the game in Vietnam—which, of course, was never in Nixon's mind, though Humphrey appeared less firm about it—the President-to-be must not paint himself into a corner in advance or make it appear to the world that he was a prisoner of his own campaign rhetoric.

Nixon had long since shed his bad past; in 1968 and then in the early years, certainly, of his Presidency the country became fully aware of this as he proceeded, both at home and abroad, to become himself what can only be called a Responsible-nominate. Unlike all the others dealt with in this work, whose whole long records are now done and sealed, his is an unfinished story about which nothing flatly and finally and without qualification can be said while a future and then an ending are yet to unfold.

Nixon, in short, had to find and did find from a painful process of trial and error and defeat and triumph what was innate with the Responsibles-elect herein saluted. This is an automatic cutoff valve. They did not need to consult it; it told them, without any pause to check the dials, when it was time to ease off the pressure. The valve throbbed quietly away in John Kennedy; in Dwight Eisenhower; in Senator Robert Taft; in Harry Truman, who had far more bitter and remorseless enemies; in Lyndon Johnson, who had even more. In these and in every other Responsible, past and present, living or dead, the valve has signaled to them not some copybook message about how one played the game; it has told them something more sophisticated and complicated, and real and true. It has told them that this is by theory and in fact a pluralistic society, legally a union of states and humanly and actually a great merger of peoples and interests, of races and religions, of pressures and counterpressures, of affirmations and of denials, of arguments

9

and rebuttals. It has told them that such a nation, that such a people, is not long to be led without its consent and that enduring consent is not to be given to a leader whose victories are too costly, whose tactics are too muscular, whose rhetoric may rise from passing anger in understandably excited combat to an unforgettable and unforgivable extremity of passion, of accusation or of recrimination.

Nixon himself later in his career looked back ruefully upon the years of the great divisiveness which he had seemed to symbolize, if not always justly so, when, as a member of the House and then of the Senate, he had sometimes appeared to equate disagreement with evil purpose. That he had never really done so did not alter the fact that many had believed he had done so. And so it required the passage of eight years—eight years of manifest civility by Richard Nixon in politics—to bring him amnesty from the public and himself to the White House.

Again, the first sharp decline in the popularity rating of Robert F. Kennedy in 1967 beyond doubt resulted from a public sense that his "feud" with President Johnson had been pressed too long and too unfairly. The people know very well that the game is supposed to be rough, and they generally enjoy the sight of a big and powerful personality taking a licking. They do not, however, like to see the beating go on too long, even though they still measure what is fair punishment for politicians on a far less charitable scale than for men in other occupations.

The reaction is commonly called sympathy for the

underdog, but it is a good deal less simplistic. For the public senses what the Responsible grasps clearly and exactly: that not only a community of interest in palpable terms but also a certain communion of joint sympathy going beyond material interest must exist, however imperfectly, between the leaders and the led.

The Responsibles themselves do, of course, at times think of revenge for real or fancied wrongs in the bear pit. But then they will drop the notion, not because they are angelic but simply because it is an inoperable notion. At best it is irrelevant to their designs; at worst it is destructive to them.

Military analogies are in many ways applicable to the Responsibles, since theirs is after all a job of leadership with some of the requirements of command itself. In military action the most delicate and difficult decisions involve the questions of when to attack, when to retreat, when only to wait. The use of too much force may be as grave an error as the use of too little. What is demanded of the commander is an instinct for the apt employment of the right degree of power at the right time, so that nothing important is lost by a policy of not-enough and so that nothing important is callously wasted by a policy of too-much.

Similarly vital is the perception of the indispensable as distinguished from the merely desirable objective. So it is with the Responsibles. They are Responsibles because they know one objective from another. They need no handbook to tell them when to commit themselves, and all they may have, to a political aim and when not to do so. Their standard is this: Is the objective big enough to justify risking much? Is it truly national in scope and meaning, or is it parochial or regional? Is it an objective, in short, that truly engages the national safety, honor or welfare? Or does it define a problem that no doubt in an ideal world ought to be settled but yet can really be deferred without vast harm to the republic?

Different times will, of course, give differing answers to these critical questions. Harry Truman was a supreme example of the Responsible notwithstanding that his domestic leadership, and indeed his leadership of the political party he was supposed to head, was at no point really effective. The famous twenty-one-point program of domestic welfare legislation, which he offered soon after he had succeeded the dead Franklin Roosevelt in 1945, lay inert in Congress from the day he sent it up to the day he left the White House, a man scorned by millions in this country but valued by more millions abroad who had little concern for what Truman had *not* done in the United States but held a respect amounting to reverence for his achievements across the world.

Too, he left his Democratic party in an undeniable mess, as a domestic political instrumentality. He was never able to control either that party or, for that matter, his own White House staff. As to the former, a partisan organization that had been matchlessly powerful in the days of Roosevelt became under Truman a quarreling shambles, split both vertically and horizontally by a screeching sense of futility and by gross organizational ineptitude. As to the latter, petty scandal of no historical importance reached into the very White House. There were tales of deep freezers given to high officials and of a mink coat handed over to a female stenographer.

But in the larger sense none of this mattered much. For circumstance had brought Truman to power at a time when not an extension of domestic welfarism but rather the control and containment of the vast enigmas of a cold war in a new age called "atomic" was the inescapable and unprecedented mission of the United States, and thus of its current leader. Here was a man who had risen from the seamy ward politics of Kansas City to be hurled into the most dangerous, the most complex and the most unknowable time for statesmen since statesmanship had begun. It mattered little as to what he could do, or did do, about his twenty-one points or about something called the Democratic party. It mattered transcendentally what he could do, and did do, about perils to mankind that were unutterable and immeasurable.

If it was an era of danger beyond previous knowledge, it was also one of splendor. The "little man" from Missouri had to face it all with no real experience in anything approaching high and arcane statecraft and with no true coaching from his fallen chief, Franklin Roosevelt. Truman was widely thought to be one of the most limited, most parochial, politicians ever to reach the Presidency. He was fully aware, so it was said at the outset, of the grubby mechanics of grubby local politics, and so perhaps he would deal skillfully with a Congress similarly schooled. But in the grand affairs of the world he would surely be altogether lost.

All these estimates, perfectly logical on the test of his past, were to collapse in disarray in the face of the one reality that had not been apprehended. This was that

Harry Truman, Kansas City and all, was a true Responsible, a true son of the spirit of paradox which makes the Responsible, however superficially a common man, a most uncommon man indeed.

It is not always true that a statesman is only a dead politician. It is sometimes true that a man becomes a great politician because he waives a pedestrian practice of the art in behalf of an inspired performance lifting that art and himself above routine response and ritualistic observance of custom. Is the Responsible, then, at his highest moments only a little less than the angels? Good God, no. On his very best day he is a man of fallibility and weakness. It is only that he has the capacity in moments of utter crisis to rise above the ordinary, in himself and in his profession, and so to acquit himself far better than his ordinary self deserves and far better than the people are ever likely to recognize. It is his occupational disability; it is, indeed, his fate often to accomplish his best in an atmosphere of public noncomprehension. To do right is not always, or even much of the time, to seem to do right. Duty may often wear an unfamiliar, even a masked, face. To accompany duty to the end is sometimes to walk alone—except, that is, for duty itself.

Take Harry Truman again. Endlessly to be rebuffed in Congress on home affairs, he never lost a single inning there on foreign affairs, and he recorded giant accomplishments: the salvation of the Mediterranean Basin from a hitherto galloping Soviet engulfment of much of Balkan Europe; the rescue of Western Europe from ruin and chaos, and the protection of Western Europe from an encroaching Russian military shadow; the maintenance against Soviet siege of the Allied lodgment in a Berlin left isolated by the war settlements; the raising up of the shield of the North Atlantic Treaty Organization, the soundest and most truly sophisticated act of creative statesmanship of his time; the first brave implementation of the new concept of collective security, in the brilliant, if tragically costly, intervention in Korea; and on and on and on.

All this Truman did, grumpily determined, belittled and undervalued, because he knew how to discriminate between objectives and understood their relative values. And in the doing of it all he calmly forfeited the game in home affairs, hitting back lustily at his detractors but never running the risk of wholly alienating them on the one aspect of matters that he *knew* must at all cost not be weakened. This was the resolute maintenance of a position of American strength in the outer world.

Not only did he concede the contest in home affairs, and forfeit his effective leadership of a party he had no time, or heart, in the circumstances, to coddle and direct. He also, and knowingly, forfeited all chance for re-election in 1952 because he had put first things first, had carried out his obligations as a Responsible while lesser men with larger vocabularies and more polished manners were pleading with him to "bend a little" to domestic outcries.

Harry Truman, like all the Responsibles, would trim with the best of them when the issue involved was trimmable without loss of irreplaceable national principle or interest. But he would grant no concession to "politics" when what was before him was in the tradition of total national necessity. He did not mind demagoguing it up, as the political pros put it, when demagoguing it up was only a question of doing small harm on some comparatively small matter. But he would retreat no inch to public pressure, not even to the ordinary partisan necessities, when he knew that his last, unalterable duty was to stand firm upon a course, no matter who, or how many, did not like that course. (Thus, Lyndon Johnson in Vietnam.)

And this is the greatness of the Responsibles. They can be as partisan as the next fellow, or even more so, when partisanship can do their party some good and the national interest no great or lasting harm. But just as they know when to shut off the valve regulating attacks upon adversaries, they know when small politicking is impermissible demagoguery.

So it is that another characteristic of the Responsibles is to be instantly responsive to public pressure where the issue is domestic comfort, and to be utterly resistant to public pressure where the matter concerned is vast—say, national safety or the integrity of national institutions or traditions.

Indeed, the stereotype of the politician as forever willing to give away cardinal principle or to compromise important truth in his lust for popularity is absurdly inapplicable to the Responsibles. In these instances they are adamantine, far more so than other professional men as a class or businessmen as a group.

Harry Truman resolutely kept in office the most maligned Secretary of State in history, Dean Acheson, fully knowing that to behead Acheson would instantly improve his standing in the polls and with his fellow Democratic politicians. Why? Not because Truman had a death wish or a hero syndrome, but simply because he knew Acheson to be honorable and competent and, far more important, that to sacrifice him to know-nothingism would be to stain an institution which had been lent to Truman's care—the institution of the Presidency of the United States.

Again, there is the memory of a war in Vietnam which American hawks found unsatisfactory because American military action was too limited and which American doves found insupportable because a President, Lyndon Johnson, would not devise some clever means to run out without quite ever saying that this was what was being done. This was the same President who sought public consensus on domestic affairs with a desperate constancy only to make his critics constantly desperate by his absolute refusal to let some consensus of weakness on foreign affairs find him an escape hatch from Vietnam.

The care and fostering of that which is really indispensable in public life: this, again, is the Responsible's hallmark. I recall Robert A. Taft of Ohio slowly and gallantly dying of cancer on the very floor of the United States Senate but never turning away for a moment from what he conceived to be his last obligatory act on this earth: to find for the Republican party, as its leader in the Senate, a man worthy of the post and able to carry it, and thus to leave a proper legacy to the Senate itself. Taft was a prudent man setting aside a solid estate for his children. It was William F. Knowland of California whom Taft chose in the end, and not because he always agreed with Knowland but rather because he had found in Knowland those qualities of stability and human decency which the Responsibles seek and sense in others.

Partisan warriors surely they are, within the limits already noted here. But haters they never are. And haters they rarely elevate in any way if they can help it. To return to military analogy, the best combat troops are rarely those who most volubly detest the enemy but rather those pros who, long blooded in action, go quietly about the killing but waste no time in calling down biblical maledictions upon their adversaries. The Southern military captain Robert E. Lee called the Yankee enemy "those people." Field Marshal Montgomery referred to the Germans as "the other chaps."

So it is, in politics, with the Responsibles. They dislike the moralistic tendency of the political amateur to see his partisan antagonists as desperately bad fellows and shrilly to call upon his own leaders to get in there and fight, in season and out of season, for reasons which on less excited analysis are less than overwhelming. Thus, the business of characterizing perfectly decent, if somewhat troublesome, Republicans as figures of sinister machinations, a kind of devil-making much practiced by some of his junior associates in his administration, always both amused and annoyed President John F. Kennedy. So did similar efforts to picture him as endlessly suffering treasonable betrayal at the hands of those dreadful fellows, the Southern Democrats.

The Responsibles, that is to say, fear and flinch from all forms of extremism, recognizing extremism, in whatever form, as the implacable enemy of a rational and effective politics. John Kennedy, for illustration, could never bring himself gladly to associate with fringe groups such as Americans for Democratic Action, not because he thought them evil but because he thought them foolishly and embarrassingly emotive.

The fringe groups repel the Responsibles, because they proceed, whether from the left or the right, on a hot-gospel conviction filled with undue love for those seen as the good guys and with undue animosity for those seen as the bad guys. To the Responsibles the unwisdom of hating too much is matched by the unwisdom of loving too much. Emotionalism in public affairs makes them uncomfortable because the fire that burns very bright in approval can burn far too high in disapproval. For this reason the common run of them—perhaps oddly, at first glance—are not profoundly effective public speakers. The phrase of blinding or wounding brilliance will occur much more often to their speech writers than to them; nearly every one of the great Responsibles I have known has been, in his own tongue and his own pen, more nearly laconic than eloquent; more nearly clipped than verbally unshorn and outgoing. Few are truly "literary." In fact, the most literary President of modern times, Woodrow Wilson, never reached the plateau of Responsibility, just as the most literary of our early national life, Thomas Jefferson, does not stand so high on the tests of wisdom and performance as does the rhetorically more spare James Madison. Jefferson and Wilson both talked a better game than they ever played. The Responsible knows that his job is only very rarely to "make the Eagle scream"; it is usually the infinitely more important job of keeping the Eagle flying strong and right.

John Kennedy, to be sure, had some earned note as a writer, but any complete examination of his writings will show that his diction was slimmed down and basically calm and, like most Responsibles, he carefully avoided overstatement.

The most moving passage in all the Presidential messages of Lyndon Johnson, which occurred in his first full address to Congress on civil rights, was moving for its simplicity alone and was in fact ad-libbed after the prepared address had run its course through the teleprompter.

"Communication" to the Responsible does not in the smallest way mean what it means to the advertising business or even to most other professions. It is rarely designed to be an exchange of ideas and thoughts, in the ordinary sense, between leader and led. It is often only nominally meant to define an existent situation or problem or point of view. Quite often it is really meant to reach into the future over the back of the present, to begin to work the soil of public opinion in an ostensible exploration of currently difficult issues against the foreseen onset of even less tractable problems which the leader has seen looming out ahead. He may be talking of one thing and thinking of a quite different thing. For the Responsible is sometimes both an expositor in the open and a prophet in secret—a prophet whose role is cautiously hidden. Reticence in power replaces the unrestrained search for power on the hustings. Nowhere in life is there so vast a gulf between pursuit and possession as in the pursuit and then the possession of high public office. No man in politics can reach the status of true responsibility unless he can wholly abandon the techniques of the pursuit once he has attained the possession.

As to that form of "communication" directly involving press relationships, many perfectly competent journalists believe that the press conference is an irreplaceable institution because it is of so much help to the politician in determining, from the questions put to him, what is in the minds of his constituents. Actually, its real value is quite something else. The Responsible—particularly in the Presidency, with its matchless apparatus for the gathering and the evaluation of political intelligence of all kinds—almost always knows very well what his constituents are thinking. The press conference does not tell him what he already knows.

What it does is to give him an opportunity, from an immense sounding board, to reply over the shoulders of the reporters to his distant critics within the large public mass: to persuade them at best; to placate them at median; to tell them what he is doing and why and, under hard and extreme necessity, to tell them the equivalent of go to hell, if in a way so decorous as softly to mask the hard, fixed purpose that lies underneath. The press conference, moreover, is a splendid device for telling adversaries in public office—those in Congress, for instance—where they, too, may go. It is a device universally used by the Responsibles, simply because it uniquely meets their needs—to lead without avoidable abrasiveness; to admonish without mortally offending the antagonist, and above all without denying to him that dignity which is indispensable to him. Many a message ostensibly addressed to only a roomful of correspondents is meant, in fact, for entirely other people, say up on Capitol Hill, and it can be received by these real targets without public loss of face since there is, so to speak, "nothing personal in it."

When John Kennedy, for example, once observed at his press conference that he was "reading more and enjoying it less," he was referring to men outside as well as inside the American publishing industry. He was in fact referring more to dissident elected Democrats who were giving him more trouble of great substance than he cared to acknowledge directly. It was a sensible form of reticence in a forum widely assumed to be one of eager disclosure.

Senator Robert A. Taft was anything but a favorite of the working press, not because he was hostile to it but simply because a good deal of what the press asked him was awkward to reply to in his circumstances. The chief of these questions was whether he was actually serving as a kind of one-man steering committee for the entire Republican party in Congress—and at some political junctures outside Congress as well. He dared not admit to the full nature of his brief lest he put other Republican noses out of joint. He had to choose between the desirable and the flatly necessary in objectives. To him and in his circumstances, the press had to come in a bad second to his overriding need to stand constant sentinel, sometimes alone, over a divided and trauma-ridden party.

Actually, and in summary, the Responsibles as a class are not exceptionally good propagandists in the usual meaning of that term except that successes in performance are good propaganda. Propaganda-making is in any case only *one* of the tools of effective politics and not necessarily even a main tool. Obviously, the science is not to be sneered at; obviously it has helped many a man to political office. The crucial point, however, is that arriving at political office is a very different thing from becoming responsibly effective in office, and it is this quite distinct latter test that determines whether a politician is in truth a Responsible.

Widespread current fears that the burgeoning of instant communications—sometimes demonstrably accompanied by instant nonthought—will bring to power a whole race of meretricious politicians are thus considerably overstated. A pleasing countenance on television is surely an asset—on the way up. But no amount of television "coverage," however kind to the subject and however uncritical, can make a man a *good* politician. There are no cosmetic lights down where the real work is done, the real decisions are made, and the men are with bland remorsefulness separated from the boys.

. . .

BOOK TWO

Harry S. Truman

• • •

He was a man of an almost aggressive absence of all outer distinction: neither tall nor short, neither stout nor thin, neither rich nor poor, neither ignorant nor learned—except in history, which he taught to himself. He was enormously patient, and quickly and violently impatient. He was religious, in a kind of backwoods Baptist way; and he could curse with a casual monotony; could drink whiskey, if moderately, and play poker and tell smutty stories with an unabashed use of the dreariest of all the four-letter words. About his person he habitually gathered two kinds of men—the ablest, the most sensitive and in every sense the best; and the dullest, the most callous and in nearly every sense the worst.

Seen in some lights and at some times, he was the very archetype of middle-class, middle-continent America; an aging, enormously commonplace fellow, metaphorically and sometimes actually wearing his American Legion overseas cap. He was never at home in the somewhat self-consciously sophisticated Atlantic seaboard, a section that was never to know him at all, as he was never really to know it at all. And yet he was alien, too, in the real and human sense, to the hearty and earthy Midwest, as in truth he was only an uncomprehending and uncomprehended outlander in a South toward which, through his Southern-born mother, he always maintained a sentimental and wistful attachment that was never reciprocated.

For the longer part of his life he was—measured against the harsh imperatives of the American success fixation—a failure or, at best, a pedestrian mediocrity dreaming no large dreams and casting the gray aura of a tired pilgrim plodding through the pervasive ordinariness that surrounds most lives at all times in all ages. When greatness fell upon him and in some wholly improbable way he was able to grasp it, to keep it and at last even to ennoble it, it descended, in his unalterably routine vocabulary of imagery, only like "a load of hay from a barn loft." This was about the best he could do to express himself spontaneously; and no matter how long or how hard he labored on occasions when he had plenty of time to express himself, he rarely finished with anything more memorable in the way of "communication."

And yet this man, this Harry Truman from Independence, Missouri, this grayish type in his glistening eyeglasses over a square and classically unmemorable face, was to become one of the very great Presidents of the United States, one of the finest masters of grand affairs and one of the most inept handlers of petty affairs and problems within the lifetime, to now, of this republic.

He was an Abraham Lincoln utterly without the melancholy grandeur of his prairie predecessor and totally lacking in the mystical quality of that gaunt, richly neurotic figure. And yet where Lincoln saved a nation, Truman saved a world.

Harry Truman was an abler President, on the whole, when things really and enduringly mattered, if only history will consult the facts and not linger overlong upon its agreeable legends, than his patron and chief, Franklin D. Roosevelt, had ever been. But again he had none of Roosevelt's exterior largeness, surely none of Roosevelt's sparkling human chemistry of charm and grace and, most oddly, certainly none of Roosevelt's tactile skill for politics as a science in and for itself. In some ways and at some times he was something of a Lyndon Johnson; and yet he never had, on his best day, the intuitive skill for public affairs of this most truly professional of all Presidents.

Looking back upon it all it could be said without undue fancifulness that Harry S. Truman's accidental elevation to the Presidency was coincident with a circumstantial change of profound meaning in the institution of the Presidency itself. For it was to turn out that beginning with Truman's era, the very nature of the Presidency, and specifically the nature of its overriding challenges, was itself to be fundamentally altered for all the foreseeable future.

Though Roosevelt had perforce led this nation into the war and very largely through it as well, the central meaning of his long tenure had all the same been domestic, and he himself was an abler leader in home terms than he ever was in world terms. Taking nothing away from his great contributions to the defeat of Fascism, the bottom truth is that his crucial tests and his crucial concerns had been in the domestic areas. He had fought the Great Depression of the thirties; he had remade the social, the economic and the political fabrics of his country. He had set in motion a homogenization of the American society that had vast but still largely domestic implications. This man, who had so long and in equally extravagant terms been both saluted and condemned as the Great Innovator of America, would in time's longer reaches be more correctly seen as its Great Conservator.

And the successor, Truman, who entered office as the very model of the parochial politician, would become in fact *the* Innovator in something far bigger than a national scene, in an earth undergoing cataclysmic change. There is a pseudo spiritual in which it is said that He—meaning God—has got the whole world in his hands. It may be tasteless, but it is not at any rate irreverent to say that as matters turned out the departure from life of the privileged and patrician Roosevelt was to leave the whole world, in secular terms, very largely in the humble, the untried, the abashed but determined hands of the very unpatrician man who was Harry Truman.

My own first sight of this man came on an April evening, along about dusk. I had walked across the Capitol from the Senate to slip into a small, hideaway office maintained by Speaker of the House Sam Rayburn of Texas and called by him, in rare moments of joviality, "the Board of Education." The Board was a watering place for such of the Speaker's friends as came more or less regularly to it in the late afternoons by a sort of invitation by osmosis. As I entered the Board of Education on this day, a compact, ordinary man in a white hat a good deal bigger than the Eastern variety of headgear and a good deal smaller than, say, the Montana version was walking rapidly out, his face slightly flushed and his hands held rather stiffly. It would, at that moment, not have been unreasonable to suppose that he had had a drink too many. But it turned out that this was very far from the case. For I saw that Rayburn was sitting at one of the high windows, looking out upon the gathering dusk and, incredibly and shockingly, tears were running down his tough cheeks.

"What in God's name . . ." I started to ask.

Rayburn turned abruptly and said, "The Boss is dead."

"And that man who just went out?" I asked.

"That's Harry; that's the President of the United States," Rayburn replied.

I had heard, of course, of Senator Truman and of Vice-President Truman, but to one only lately returned from long absence in the war this was a name but not a face and not really an identity. Truman, of course, was going down to the White House to take up a burden which he had never remotely expected to shoulder. It was a burden for which he had in no way been prepared by Roosevelt, and a burden from whose frightening weight he openly flinched in his first days and weeks, with that strange mixture of genuine humbleness of spirit and combative pride and resolution which would never leave him in the nearly eight urgent years that had now begun.

In those first weeks and months the country understood too well the depth of his humility. But the country quite missed the extraordinary strength and the laconic courage and unassuming wisdom that lay beneath the surface of his personality. The critics, the politicians and most of the public had seen but one side of his coin; and the resulting oversimplifications were to pursue him to the end. For he had come in tabbed, in a kind of shorthand that is peculiarly American, as a "simple man," a "common man." And though he was both, in a superficial, cliché way, he was neither in any way that really mattered. The Truman of the simple slogans, the one-dimensional slogans that were as unaware of reality as were the old balloonized words in the comic strips, was to be forever at war, in many minds, with the Truman that really was.

To recollect now those early days of the new administration is to remember a scene more of pathos than of drama: The new President learning for the first time that something later to be called the atom bomb was being prepared in the crypts of Tennessee; the new President scrabbling about among such papers of state as he could find to try to learn what had really been going on all over the world and, even more poignantly, what had really been planned, and with whom, by his dead predecessor; the new President meeting for the first time, apart from previous handshakes at some cocktail party or the other, the great figures of an administration that was dead and yet must still go on; the new President taking the measure of these and other men—Harry Hopkins, Henry Stimson, Averell Harriman, and so on—who had heretofore to him been cardboard caricatures whose faces and whose doings he had really seen only in the press—this was a gingerly, a shy and a frightfully worried new President, who would sit patiently at night to write letters to "Mama," and to his sister, Mary, like a tourist from South Dakota writing back home of the wonders of the city of Washington. Neither the political nor the nonpolitical literature of this country was ever enriched by these letters from Harry to the folks back home in Missouri, but any sensitive reading of them in the afterlight is in another sense a rewarding experience indeed. For like Harry Truman himself they were on two levels: simple and small-towny and almost pastoral on the one level and powerfully illustrative, on the other, of a developing Presidency which would find its holder more than adequate to the new demands that would make that office the powerhouse of many nations rather than principally only of one, and the focal point of fateful decision for the future of more than half the human race.

For as Harry Truman took his pen in hand to write to Mama and to Mary, he half-consciously was presiding over a quantitative and qualitative mutation in that office which for the first time would require the subordination of every sheerly national interest to faraway and endlessly competing interests in a world broken in body and maddened in spirit by trial and danger.

Had Roosevelt lived on, of course, this sea change in the institution of the Presidency—in its pressures, in its obligations and in its real mandates—would in any event have occurred. Truman's accession did not create the change; it coincided with a historical process now moving at high acceleration as the war was drawing to a close in Europe and was approaching its climax in Asia.

There was, nevertheless, a sort of biblical irony of paradox—the first shall be last, the last shall be first—in the circumstance that the most significant alteration in the nature of the Presidency in all its history, an alteration making it truly magesterial over the fortune of many lands rather than essentially only over one, reached its completion in a new and accidental incumbent whose entire experience had been with what was relatively small rather than what was large in public affairs.

For Harry S. Truman had entered politics upon the sufferance, the favor and the patronage of one of the last and one of the most parochial of the old time political bosses, "Big Tom" Prendergast of Kansas City, Missouri. And, being Harry Truman, he never sought to conceal and never was willing remotely to apologize for these far-from-grand beginnings. To the end he refused to heed the appeals of fellow Democrats of the "new" or reform coloration to disown old "Big Tom." Indeed, President of the United States though he had now become, he attended Prendergast's funeral in 1945 and let the editorial writers howl in moral fury, as they howled against him on many other occasions for his unshakable loyalty to the bad fellows whom it was his equally unshakable habit to know and to like.

The Truman story from the outset was an Andy Jackson sort of story quite shorn of the derring-do and of the glamour that attached itself to Old Hickory. Not a chemical trace of glamour was granted by fate to the man who was in impersonal political terms but never in personal terms the twentieth century's Andrew Jackson. It was no accident that Harry Truman's most splendid ejaculation of profanity—and the only one he ever used that was not banal and highly unexceptionable—was the splendid cry: "Jesus Christ and Andy Jackson!" This striking call was employed by Truman whenever an event was both highly stirring and highly unexpected; whenever circumstances had got him into some corner that was both tight and elating to his martial spirit; or simply whenever the trials and dangers of his world and time had left him otherwise speechless and troubled— but never afraid.

The Harry Truman who set out upon a public career at the beginning of the nineteen-twenties was not a man who could pick and choose. Though he had never been able to go to college, and had been prevented by nearsightedness from seeking the appointment to one of the service academies that had been his boyhood hope, he was nevertheless able in the First World War to earn a commission as a first lieutenant and eventually become a captain of artillery. He fought in the St.-Mihiel and Argonne offensives— perhaps the best-known engagements to involve American troops—but when he came back home he had nothing in view. With an old Army friend he set up a men's clothing store—the famous "haberdashery" that later became an anti-Truman taunt both to snob Democrats and to honestly malicious partisan Republicans—and straightaway ran it into the ground. It went broke, and left Truman $20,000 in debt. He refused to plead bankruptcy; and it took him ten years to pay off his obligations.

When the haberdashery shut its doors for the last time —no doubt still piteously featuring in its windows the too-gay togs which Harry Truman himself resolutely always wore to the horror of aesthetes in apparel—Tom Prendergast came along and found Harry S. Truman. Prendergast was continuously under valid criticism for associates who would now be called baddies, and many of these baddies were Catholic in religion and "foreign" in ethnic origin. Truman's sturdily Baptist, Masonic, American Legion background was rightly estimated by Prendergast to be an asset, as were Lyndon Johnson's personal data similarly useful in 1960 to John F. Kennedy.

Under Prendergast's sponsorship Truman became, successively, Overseer for Highways of Jackson County (Kansas City), Presiding Judge (nonlegal) of the County Court, and United States Senator from Missouri. The Senate became Truman's favorite home, as he saw it and as he often put it. It is, however, an awkward fact that the Senate never quite reciprocated by regarding Harry Truman as *its* best and favorite member—or even the next-next-best or next-favored. For Truman never entered a Senate institution of the spirit which this writer once denominated as the Inner Club. He lacked those all but indefinable qualities of casual leadership which are the keys to the club, keys as gossamer as moonlight and yet as real and as strong as steel. The truth is that as a Senator he was what the collegians of a generation ago called a grind. The other Senators came to "like Harry," but somehow he lacked the spark—of grace, of charm, of whatever. And he worked too hard and, on the whole, perhaps too humorlessly.

His career in the Senate was in fact without distinction, except for his work as chairman of a wartime special committee set up to watch over the rearmament and defense programs. Truman's contributions here—for efficiency, against graft and boondoggling—were enormous. He had come up from a political way of life which was wise indeed in the uses of graft and gravy, though his own reputation in this regard was never once compromised or successfully challenged. The Senate could not have had a better man to do this job; and eventually, even amid the overcast of the great and terrible events of that time, "the Truman committee" entered the consciousness of the influentials of this nation, and Truman himself became a man at least to watch if not to reckon with. This accomplishment was authentically Trumanesque. It was largely without benefit of the sweet—and sometimes oversweet if not actually decadent—uses of publicity. It was a plodding, honest and self-deprecating job. But no absence of the kudos so readily obtained by other Senators was able at length totally to hide it from public view.

The chairman of the Truman committee thus found himself one day, to his surprise, to be a figure whose writ ran beyond Missouri; and this circumstance was not lost upon the man then in the White House. In the wartime Democratic Convention of 1944 Franklin D. Roosevelt, personally a little tired of his then Vice-President, Henry A. Wallace, and also alive to the opinion of others that Wallace was altogether too uncritically sympathetic to the Soviet Union, played a cool game of kingmaking or, more exactly, of princemaking.

Roosevelt pondered over alternatives to Wallace, and two names were really in the running—that of Truman and that of Supreme Court Justice William O. Douglas. The Presidential nod at length fell, in benign absentmindedness, upon Harry S. Truman—who had the support, in an instance of historical appropriateness, of the principal bosses of the Democratic party. Truman accepted the honor with throat-gulping simplicity—a simplicity that was a very long way from that simple-mindedness which many were forever to attribute to him. To the assembled Democratic Convention delegates he made an address that was equally in character.

"You don't know how very much I appreciate the great honor that has come *to the State of Missouri*. It is also a great responsibility *which I am perfectly willing to assume*. . . . I don't know what else I can say except that I accept this great honor *with all humility*." To examine this bit of less-than-shining rhetoric is to see in a few words the two sides to Harry Truman; both entirely genuine; both easily subject to underestimation and undervaluation. What might be called the humility of Harry was utterly real. But no less real was that other phrase: ". . . *which I am perfectly willing to assume*."

Roosevelt had got himself a Vice-President who would surely do as he was told, and nothing that he was not told to do. But he had not got what his behavior toward Truman, in the brief weeks in which Truman was only Vice-President, indicated that he supposed he had got:

simply an embodied Missouri Compromise to still and placate the restive ideological crosscurrents and competing private ambitions within the Democratic party. For the chemistry of Harry Truman was an odd thing. He was a politician who said no more than he meant, but also no less than he meant. And he was also in a quiet, offhand way a striking illustration of the truth of what another great leader, Winston Churchill, once observed: that the British race had not crossed every ocean and desert and mountain chain of this earth because it was made of sugar candy.

Moreover, the home reading that had been Harry Truman's prep school and university, while Roosevelt was elegantly tooling along at Groton and still more elegantly later at Harvard, had offered to him a rigorous self-tutoring in which the history of men and nations was the dominant theme. Truman, that is to say, knew vastly more than anybody—and most of all Roosevelt—ever supposed, or even faintly suspected. Indeed, lese majesty though it be, he knew more about history than did Franklin Roosevelt or any other contemporary statesman but for Winston Churchill.

This, to be sure, was no log-cabin superhero. Nor was there in him some tremolo vindication of that sanctified legend in which the lad from the wrong side of the tracks storms the world of the big banks and high society and makes good in both. For Truman was of quite satisfactory "old-family" background. It was simply that like many men of his circumstances and generation, what used to be called "The Advantages" had not been open to him.

The first of the postwar depressions, that of the early twenties when the first of the Red Hot Mammas were heating up only to meet at last the chill dawn with Dead Broke Daddies, had finished the process of making him a hybrid form of Jeffersonian Democrat who agreed with the Master in sentiment but in little else. He was, that is to say, something of what the more extreme right-wing critics were always pleased to call a giveaway type of politician. He honestly despised and feared such folklore ogres as "Wall Street" and the "Eastern Bankers," some of whose outstanding exemplars he was at length gladly to employ in his administration, along with some undeniably "Wall Street Lawyers."

But, again, all this was only a part of Harry S. Truman. For the same President who made a pass, at least, at being a "spender" in the Roosevelt model was also as tough as any country banker about money itself, though he never was able to convince the conservatives of this fact. As a budget-maker in the White House he was said by one of his associates, and in simple truth, to "know where every goddamn dime is—and why it's there." And while in the social welfare sense he was a liberal, he was never that very different fellow who is a reformist liberal. He never supposed that any domestic problem, whether housing or more economic security or even civil rights, could stand upon equal footing with this nation's awful mission to defend first itself and then all those associated nations which, as the Second World War drew toward its end, were left lying naked and starving before the new, post-czarist expansionism of Russia under Joseph Stalin—of whom Harry Truman was once to say most incautiously: "I like Old Joe."

Where Roosevelt, though far from blind to the latent menace, had nevertheless believed he could handle Old Joe's postwar Russia, and thus had made unwisely trusting accommodations with the Soviets over Europe that had deeply concerned Churchill, cold skepticism touched Truman from his first days in the White House. Perhaps it was because he himself had come up the hard way, a way that the privileged Roosevelt could apprehend intellectually but not viscerally. At any rate, Harry Truman, devoted as he was to Roosevelt's tenure and memory and pledged as he was from the beginning to carry on the Roosevelt policies as best he could, was compelled very shortly to brood anxiously upon the implications of those policies as they had to do with a Cold War already developing. As he had been able without the slightest trouble to sense and smell a bad apple in the war defense barrel, Truman began right away to sniff in concern the odor rising from Stalin's increasingly ominous attitudes toward the Allied arrangements made first by Roosevelt at the Yalta Conference and second by the worriedly raw and green world statesman named Truman at the Potsdam Conference.

Never having been in any real way taken into confidence by Roosevelt about anything—not so much because Roosevelt wished to depreciate Truman as simply because he had a war on—the new President had come to office with no relevant information that had not been the common property of the newspapers and radio.

Never had any man confronted such frightful responsibilities and burdens with so little in the way of the antecedent facts. Still, Truman dared not reveal to the nation or to the world the depth of his involuntary ignorance, for his stoutly traditional view of the majesty of the Presidential office left no room, here or ever afterward, for any concession that the *Presidency*, as distinguished from the man named Truman who occupied it, could be short of either data or of decisiveness.

His first decision, accordingly, was to direct that the seed conferences in San Francisco which were to set up the United Nations should go forward, as had been planned by Roosevelt, in April of 1945, even though he had not been involved at all in the long administration studies that had preceded the fixing of date and place and agenda. This was done in the first meeting of the Truman Cabinet, and at its conclusion Secretary of War Henry L. Stimson lingered behind to tell the President of "an immense project that was under way." This, as Truman has recalled in his memoirs, was a bit of a thing called the atomic bomb.

At the time of the preparations for San Francisco, however, the American, British and Soviet armies were about to make a linkage in the heart of Europe and coincident with this juncture Joseph Stalin was beginning to raise the most serious question as to whether he intended to honor the agreements made by him at Yalta and Potsdam. In briefer terms, Stalin was about to open his fateful campaign to throw Soviet hegemony from Poland westward across to the very borders of France. Ambassador Averell Harriman had come back from Moscow to tell Truman in plain words that the then widely current dream of genuine American-Soviet postwar cooperation was only a dream; that what Stalin was after was a surface "cooperation" with America and Britain behind which he would extend Soviet control in Europe as far as he could reach.

Now Truman was in a fix, indeed. On the one hand this nation and all the Western world were looking with agonized hope at an institution then only in its conceptual phase, the United Nations, which would "outlaw" war and all that. Clearly, an American rupture with Stalin's Russia at this point would shatter both the dream and those far more modest hopes for a United Nations which were both realistic and attainable. But on the other hand here was gathering evidence that Stalin had no intention of accommodating his real views to his Western Allies and no intention whatever of softening a policy of militant expansionism in Europe at the expense of the very values for which the Western Allies had fought in the contest with Hitler and Company.

It was in this poignant dilemma that Harry Truman first proved that subtlety of thought and action in the crisis arenas of world affairs which was so improbable a part of his leadership qualities, given all his background and experience. Some of his advisers urged him to go on as though nothing bad was happening in Poland and the rest of Eastern Europe, where Stalin was even then poised for a pounce of rare rapacity. For, they said in effect to the President, "after all, we must do nothing whatever to shake the delicate egg from which is to be hatched this new world agency for peace, the United Nations." Other advisers went far in the other direction and so urged the President to denounce the Russians in no uncertain terms, and so on. The first recommendation would have amounted in fact to a policy of head-in-the-sand, of see and hear no evil. The second would have amounted in fact to a policy of go-to-hell, which would have given a splendid release to Truman's mounting exasperation but which all the same would have been irresponsible in the context of all the existing realities.

Characteristically, Truman took the sober middle course. He was not about to saddle the United States of America with the vast onus of breaking the egg of the U.N. before any chick could emerge. But he was also not about to let the Russians suppose that the failed haberdasher from Missouri did not know what the Russians were doing and why. So he said to his advisers that while he knew he could hardly expect a one hundred per cent performance on their promises of Yalta and Potsdam from the Russians he would damn well demand eighty-five per cent, anyhow. There was a good deal of backing and filling—a good deal of what General George C. Marshall always called "the backs and forths"—and Truman at length told V. M. Molotov of the Soviet Union that Harry Truman knew what Stalin was up to and would not stand still for it.

Speaking specifically of Stalin's open and undeniable efforts to prevent the formation in ravaged Poland of a government of free Polish choice, rather than a Soviet satellite, Truman informed Molotov that the United States was prepared to carry out honorably all the undertakings of the Yalta Conference but demanded that the Soviet Union do the same.

"I expressed once more the desire of the United States for friendship with Russia," Truman recalled later, "but I wanted it clearly understood that this could only be on the basis of mutual observation of agreements and not on the basis of a one-way street."

"I have never been talked to like that in my life!" Molotov protested in great and genuine anger.

"Carry out your agreements," snapped Truman, "and you won't get talked to like that!"

This conversation formed a historical watershed of transcendental meaning to the world, for it signaled a determination reached then by Truman and never to be departed from in all the years ahead. He made up his mind then and there that two giant realities would govern him in foreign policy. The first was that the Russians were not to be trusted and that the American attitude toward them was henceforth to be based upon a position of resolutely maintained national strength, real but never truculent, skeptical but never cynically sterile, hopeful but never foolishly credulous. This would please the American right wing to a point, but not nearly far enough. For the Right wanted him not simply to maintain the position of strength but to carry it into an outright belligerency toward Soviet Communism that could have ended in global conflict.

The second of the realities was Truman's determination that rational suspicion of the Soviet Union's motives was not to be allowed to freeze the United States into a stance of total negativism toward the possibility, at least, of some postwar cooperation, however gingerly, between Washington and Moscow. He knew very well that in the Soviet Union he faced a power factor of ominous potentialities, but he was unwilling simply to close the door to all options save the ghastly option of irremediable hostility between the only two genuine power centers in the postwar world. Thus, in time he would offer to the Russians a participation in the American monopoly of the new nuclear devices. It was a tender of incredible generosity, for at that time the whole world, not excluding the Soviet Union, could have lain at the mercy of an America uniquely armed. But it was also a tender of great wisdom. For when the Russians rejected it out of hand they proved at that moment the essential decency of American purposes; they themselves established that a nation demonstrably able to impose its fiat across the globe had no fiat in mind, no smallest purpose to bully that globe.

Still, all this did not please the Left. For while the Right wanted a kind of absurd high noon showdown with the Russians, the Left was quite lost in its dreams of a "good" Soviet Union in an impossibly "good" world now to open out for mankind. To the Right, therefore, Truman was to be forever too "soft" on international Communism; to the Left he was forever to be too "tough."

By the time Truman had his encounter with Molotov he was having many exchanges, some by cable and some by scrambler telephone, with Winston Churchill, and the American in this high dialogue was more and more liking what he heard from the London end, and vice versa. On Truman's side in these early days there was an immense and almost religious awe of the splendidly articulate and aristocratic Churchill, not solely because of Churchill's extraordinary qualities but also because of Truman's personal humility. Still the President never forgot that he *was* President, and though his attitude was unvaryingly deferential to the Prime Minister, in it was also implicit the awareness that in power terms the Washington part of the partnership was very much the bigger and more powerful one.

Though there is no documentary proof of this, I had personal reason to believe that Churchill on his side actually had opened his association with Truman with a politely masked lack of respect for his American colleague. Churchill, too, at the start fell victim to the "little man" stereotype that had been fastened upon Truman by much of the Washington press. For the press, too, was still lost in grief over Roosevelt's death and inclined to look upon the new President as a presumptuous, and surely not graceful, outsider.

But as he began to know the Truman of actuality rather than the Truman of mythology, the Prime Minister changed on the inside an early estimate that he had never acknowledged outside. As time went on, indeed, he got along more easily with Harry Truman, and with less necessity to explain himself, than he had with Roosevelt. There were complicated reasons for this. To begin with, the Roosevelt-Churchill grand alliance was never, in personal terms, quite so close or quite so happy as most people thought at the time. There was a good deal of genuine friction in it, as some of us who were correspondents in wartime England well knew but never then advertised, for obvious reasons.

First of all, Churchill and Roosevelt differed fundamentally on high Allied strategy. Churchill wanted at all costs to keep Stalin's troops out of Central and Southern

Europe, and Roosevelt was not so much concerned about that. Churchill had the liveliest fear that the Russian devil who had been an angel when he needed Allied aid would turn to devilish pursuits again when the Nazis were kaput. Roosevelt thought that with a bit of doing here and there he could keep the devil in check and perhaps even persuade him to return at last to something approaching a democratic path.

There were, moreover, purely personal difficulties that cast some sand into the works. Roosevelt, though few Americans ever suspected it, had to my knowledge a good deal of inherited anglophobia in his purely private attitudes and, ironically, more than a trace of the perfidious-Albion syndrome he had inherited from forebears who once dueled bitterly with British mercantile interests in the China trade. Actually, he tended always slightly to patronize Churchill, as an embodiment of a dying Tory system, a Colonel Blimp, really, who meant well but had pretty well had it in the modern world. Moreover, Churchill believed in the doctrine of Original Sin in international affairs; Roosevelt had the classic liberal's total faith in the perfectibility of men and nations and international power systems.

The long and short of it was that in a purely instinctual way Truman, though himself very liberal, reached essentially Churchill's view of world affairs once he had been in the White House long enough to catch up on the realities of the game.

His original and, to be sure, rather too generous pledge simply to carry on uncritically all that Roosevelt had had in train would no doubt have been demanded of him at any rate by a country in which millions were in grief. Too, the associates in government whom he had inherited from FDR were not at this point really prepared to see him as the President. Truman, himself, for that matter, later confessed that for a good many weeks he was thinking when he used the term "the President" not of himself but rather of Franklin Roosevelt. He himself was then no different, part of the time, from most of the rest of his countrymen in feeling that Harry Truman was really only a caretaker in a mansion still alive with the memory and the spirit of a dead leader.

The rest of the time, however, Truman knew very well that this humanly understandable emotion was not one that could be allowed much scope. For the Roosevelt era had ended forever, like a parting in the rope of time, and the harsh imperatives both of personal responsibility and of history would not allow Truman to dwell overlong on a past to which as Vice-President he had been largely irrelevant at the expense of a future which was unavoidably his to master.

So it was that some five months after his inauguration, amid the transcendental problems of a war in Europe now ending and a war in Asia only reaching its climax and still very far from won, he prepared a domestic message to Congress in which he laid out a "twenty-one-point program for postwar recovery and adjustment." It was an odd document indeed. In substance it followed faithfully the domestic innovations that Roosevelt had hoped one day to accomplish but had had to put aside because of the overriding demands of war. But though the general impression at the time was that it had been

offered in all earnestness, realists found the program
difficult to take seriously in the Washington atmosphere
of those days.

Not only was the war itself engaging all the attention
of a tired Congress and a tired, snappish people; the
American mood also had no time or taste for domestic
reforms. For, among other things, the Great Depression
was even then to most people a distant memory of a
largely forgotten nightmare; and all Truman's talk of
more housing, more civil rights and so on had the emotional impact of a discussion of, say, the precise level of
the water table in the Mississippi Valley.

The American people, in short, had had a long bel-
lyfull of any form of self-denial and, indeed, of any impulse to altruism. To the extent that the war and the
looming hopes for general demobilization were not all-
preoccupying, the general civilian interests had become
crude and vulgar. The people wanted to talk about the
shortage of red meat and butter, and never mind all this
dreary business about social welfare and so on. The system of price controls that had worked pretty well while
the war in Europe stood in crisis was everywhere breaking down. Gone now was the whole spirit of a reasonable
community self-restraint that had heretofore moved the
nation.

All this Truman sensed. But he could not give this
condition of internal affairs much of his time or interest;
could take no effective measures of moral leadership
against it, because the White House was still a war and
postwar policy command post and not much else.

So it was that when he left Washington on a special

train—a deliberately old-fashioned and sedate method of transport intended to recall the country to its calm yesterdays—to go out to Missouri to vote in the 1946 Congressional elections, even the least sensitive of the passengers could feel grass-roots stirrings that boded no good for the still-new Truman administration in domestic terms. In a VIP car just next to that of Truman himself, the President's old friend, Speaker Sam Rayburn, held a melancholy seminar with such correspondents—including this writer—as dropped in. Looking grumpily out the train window at the rich harvest lying upon the fields of Ohio, Rayburn observed with a melancholy preliminary grunt, "This, you know, is going to be nothing but a goddamned beefsteak election."

Again, when the train halted at St. Louis and Missouri's gift to the Presidency stood at its rear gate to address briefly a small crowd that had gathered, no witness could have supposed that the home folks were happy with their returning son. Nor were matters improved by the characteristic action of one of those so-called—and endlessly so-called—"Truman cronies" named Major General Harry Vaughan, a Presidential military aide. Vaughan, whose manners were essentially and unhappily those of a rural deputy sheriff, expressed himself by leaping down from the train platform into the crowd and gratuitously pushing it around a bit to keep himself in training. Truman's response then said much for his persistent habit of selecting the most unfortunate, as well as the most fortunate, of associates.

He offered no rebuke to Vaughan but simply looked at him with absent tolerance and behaved as though the episode had never occurred. Vaughan would cause him much grief before it was all over, and so would other "cronies" who accepted petty but politically damaging gifts and favors. But to the end, as on that day in St. Louis, the President would cling to his human liabilities quite as firmly as to his human assets.

While this was not a unique trait among politicians— John F. Kennedy was later to find painful at times some of those friends who tagged at his elbow and so was Lyndon B. Johnson—Truman carried his faithfulness to a nostalgic past further, surely, than had any other President in our history. Like some others in this sense, and most nearly like Lyndon Johnson, he had always an essential bigness of attitude toward things that in reason and in logic were trivial but which were in political terms—in a country still strongly touched by its Puritan heritage—all too important.

Thus, he could tolerate any amount of punishment of himself but very little for his friends, even when they were wrong, and none whatever of his family. Once, when his daughter Margaret had given a singing recital in Washington, a music critic for the Washington *Post*, Paul Hume, wrote an unflattering notice. Truman, though up to his eyes with problems of world meaning, wrote to Hume a note threatening to kick him in a private part of his anatomy.

Again, his iron loyalty to those he liked had other extreme outlets. An old Army man, he took the unprecedented course on one occasion of denouncing the United States Marine Corps for being too "fancy" and too pushy. Another incident occurred at a dinner party in the home of Mr. and Mrs. William P. Bundy in celebration of the wedding anniversary of Mrs. Bundy's father, Dean Acheson, Truman's old Secretary of State, and Mrs. Acheson. HST, then in retirement, issued a crisp critique of the decisions of a special Senate committee which under the leadership of John F. Kennedy had undertaken to designate the five outstanding Senators of all time. High on this list, of course, was John C. Calhoun of South Carolina, the great exponent of the Doctrine of the Concurrent Majority. Absent from it, of course, was the faithfully Democratic but pedestrian Senator from New York, Robert F. Wagner, Sr. Truman listened with growing displeasure to a dinner-table conversation that largely endorsed the wisdom of the Kennedy selection committee. At last, unable longer to abide it all, he proclaimed to me, "For God's sake, man, why John Calhoun? Damn it all, that fellow tried to destroy the Union. And, for God's sake, why not my friend Bob Wagner?"

Others present, including the late Supreme Court Justice, Felix Frankfurter, sought in vain to point out that men were not selected as great Senators because one liked or agreed with them but only because of the creative power which for good or ill they had shown. "Ah," said Mr. Truman, "nonsense"—or rather a harsher word of that general nature.

Wagner, you see, had not only been Truman's Senate friend and partisan comrade, but also Truman's ideological associate on labor issues. The President in this little episode was speaking from that side of his character that reflected the oversimplified personal loyalties and the strongly partisan streak to which he never hesitated to give full rein in personal and purely domestic political affairs. This was the "Give 'em Hell, Harry" politician who could readily see home issues as simply and plainly the dividing factors between the good fellows and the bad fellows, much as he had done as county judge back in Missouri.

And yet the same politician, given a foreign policy issue that involved all American parties and deep national interests, was capable of an aseptically unpartisan detachment that had not been seen in the American Presidency in this century, and perhaps not ever except in the beginnings of the republic in the eighteenth century when White House occupants were not chosen by popular suffrage and thus had little reason to act demagogically.

This striking aspect of Harry Truman, this quality that made of him a great President, was entirely unknown, even to his oldest friends, until the early postwar collapse of British power, British presence and British will in the basin of the Mediterranean. This confronted the new President with the appalling challenge to world stability that ended in his proclamation of the Truman Doctrine for the salvation of Greece and Turkey from the first use by Soviet-oriented Communism of that immensely tricky technique that was later to be called a "war of liberation." The Communists, that is to say, set out in Greece and Turkey, and more critically in the former, to "liberate" the people from such faint doses of democracy as they were permitted to swallow and to hand them over with great kindness to a Communist

dictators' hegemony already bringing the unique blessings of Peoples' Republics into Eastern Europe.

This sinister business was, of course, the pilot model
for a long trail of aggression by proxy which would not
end for many years and which as this is written, indeed,
has held South Vietnam in the grip of years of torture.
That Truman precisely saw all this ahead may be debatable, but that he saw its general potentialities a generation
ago is perfectly clear.

At all events, when the Greek-Turkish crisis had
reached its apogee he called to the White House the
Congressional leaders of both parties to explain the position to them and to put before them what he intended
to do—that is, to commit American military power to
resist the gathering Communist attempt to overrun
Greece and Turkey in the name of "popular revolution."

In this meeting, as so often later he would do, he simply granted consultation to Congress. This was not because the Constitution required him to do so; because, as
he had quietly remarked upon taking his office, it was the
President's business to "make foreign policy." He
brought Congress in simply because he thought Congress had a right to know what he was about to do; not
to ask the permission of Congress for the course he was
in any case going to follow.

There was a lively discussion on the substance of the
great issue, a discussion wholly encouraged by Truman.
But then one of the delegation from Capitol Hill, most
likely the late Senator Scott Lucas of Illinois, put in a
remark: "But what about the domestic political implications of all this, Mr. President?"

Truman, as Speaker Rayburn later told me, looked up in anger and spat out, "Political implications? To hell with that. So long as I am President and so long as we are discussing a matter of this kind I don't ever want to hear those goddamn words ever mentioned here again." And so, as Rayburn remembered, those goddamn words were, indeed, never again mentioned to Truman in any conference dealing with any international crisis.

Indeed, it was Rayburn's view that of all the Presidents he had known—and these went back in time to Woodrow Wilson—none among them had ever approached foreign policy so nonpolitically as had Truman.

Not the least of the many ironies of the service of Harry Truman to his country was the fact that all this was never remotely apprehended by that country. In his role as the creator and expositor and executor of American foreign policy Truman acted simply and solely on the basis of what he thought to be right and necessary and never once counted the cost or the difficulty in domestic political terms. So it was that while he was a tireless—and joyful—partisan adversary of Republicans in domestic terms, habitually flinging at them the hot epithets over which as a boy he had glowed in the Lamar (Mo.) *Democrat*, he warmly embraced all manner of Republicans when the question before the house was internationally transcendental rather than familiar and homespun.

Republicans who were quite dreadful here at home were splendid and irreplaceable men to him in his foreign designs. And so he treasured Henry Stimson, Rob-

ert Patterson and all the other rich Republican types of
his national security establishment who came down
from the environs of Wall Street looking down their
noses at this belligerent outlander and remained to give
to him an utter devotion for his high leadership and
readily to forgive him his trespasses when on occasion he
put on his partisan hat and assailed "the interests" of
which all their lives they had been a part.

He found, as he went on, that men of his own party
were sometimes remarkably unsatisfactory, if not actively disloyal to him, when he was up against the iron
realities of the outer world. So he soon replaced his old
senior in the Senate, James F. Byrnes of South Carolina,
as Secretary of State and brought in, successively, General George C. Marshall and Dean Acheson to preside
over that center of endless crisis, that ordained lightning
rod for public displeasure and public hostility, which is
the American foreign office. Acheson, to be sure, was a
Democrat, too, but a prickly one who had been fired by
Roosevelt from a lesser job. But he was also essentially
a foreign-policy professional, as General Marshall had
been. Neither the Marshall nor the Acheson appointment was remotely political, and neither ever did Truman the slightest good in domestic terms.

The aloof Marshall, one always suspected, was at heart
a Republican, if anything, and he entered upon Truman's service, first as Secretary of State and later as
Secretary of Defense, with the air of a man putting his
foot into an odd and not very attractive house owned by
an odd man named Truman and impelled sheerly by a
sense of duty. All the same, he served Truman with a

bleak and total devotion, though to the end they were as stiff in each other's company as a pair of strangers. The General, of course, always called Truman "Mr. President"; but the President on his side never got beyond "General" in speaking to his subordinate.

It was, in any event, George Marshall who marched stolidly with the President when, after having arrested the expansion of armed Communism along the Mediterranean, he set out to rehabilitate Western Europe in what was surely the greatest act of American statesmanship and enlightened American self-interest since Roosevelt had put over Lend-Lease during the war. Characteristically sensitive to realities before others could see them, and characteristically and most improbably thinking in grand designs, Truman early reckoned that the military victory over Hitler in Europe must be followed by a victory over economic chaos, over rubble and over hunger and disease and over a political vacuum strewn with wreckage and death. So for the relief and rescue of Europe he prepared the multi-billion-dollar Marshall Plan—so named because George Marshall was its laconic spokesman in this and other countries and carried it about with him, as he once told me, "like a damn traveling salesman in a devil of a hurry."

In the meantime, however, Marshall became another symbol as well. The fall of mainland China to the Communists had dismayed and enraged much of the United States. Our arms had been the critical factor in the destruction of both the European and Japanese ends of the Fascist Axis, and for all our exertions and pains and perils here we were all the same with an evil colossus bestriding a good part of the earth in the Orient.

Marshall had not only been our principal American military leader in wartime as Chief of Staff of the Army (and this, indeed, he was, far more in the end even than General Dwight Eisenhower) but he had also been on a mission to China which had signally failed to save it from the marauding Communists. The Republicans, and particularly the right-wing Republicans, could not believe that this disaster could have occurred without American ineptitude or even American duplicity. Who, then, but George Marshall could have been the architect of this staggering tragedy—and if George Marshall, then what of his boss, Harry Truman?

So there opened in this country a bitter and a divisive debate. Violent men, intoxicated by frustration, literally maddened by frightful suspicions, and in transports of fury at what was undeniably the greatest victory for armed Communism since the Bolshevik revolution itself, set off upon a campaign, based on demonology, on the conspiracy theory of history, to destroy George Marshall, Harry Truman and whoever else could be supposed to have guilt for the death in China of the Nationalist regime headed by Chiang Kai-shek.

An embittered extremist, Senator William Jenner of Indiana, on the floor of the Senate called General George C. Marshall, the intellectual hero of the Second World War, "a front man for traitors . . . a living lie." Marshall icily ignored it all and when I told him what Jenner had said he replied in frigid tones, "Who is Senator Jenner?" Truman, for his part, sat it out with unruffled dignity in the White House, never for a moment neglecting to give

Marshall his full public and private backing, helplessly watching the development of one of the most malignant and destructive myths of American history. This was the myth that the Government of the United States was alone responsible for the fall of a corrupt, unmartial regime to a savagely fanatic and unhappily efficient Communist war machine which could never have been halted by any American administration short of a commitment dwarfing our sacrifices against both Hitler and Japan.

The Communist victory in China would for many years unfairly curse the Truman administration and unjustly stain its record, its unparalleled record, for prescient, valorous and wise action to arrest all around the globe, but for this single exception, the forces of the new aggression that had followed the death of Fascism from Tokyo to Berlin. Many would demand of Truman why he had not "saved" China; but not so many would ask him how it was that he had saved Greece and Turkey and Western Europe and the Republic of Korea. This was the nature of his Gethsemane; and the ordeal would accompany him to the very end of the long, long road which he followed with such courage, such honor and such skill as one of the great Responsibles of all time.

The issue had become embittered beyond hope, and the more it was hashed over the more hopelessly inflamed and confused it became. At last, though well aware that it was not a time or a season for rational explanations to be rationally accepted, and knowing, too, that the more the administration might say the more its critics would ignore context and select such passages as in truncated form would support their own case, Truman acted to respect the demands of future history, notwithstanding the obvious cost to his own "image." He directed the publication in 1949 of a mammoth white paper on China, which the historian Gaddis Smith thus described in 1968: "Never before or since has the American Government released such a huge and unbiased selection of inside information concerning a current controversy." But only honest history did this serve; the political effect was simply to give additional weapons to a group that was using China to kill Truman's Presidency.

The fall of China was tirelessly offered by Republican partisan extremists as a kind of proof of "softness on Communism" on the part of the most successful of the great adversaries of militant Communism the world had ever known. It was this grotesque accusation and the twin accusation of "cronyism," by which was imputed to him a conscious kinship with unworthy public figures, that became Truman's ultimate albatross and, at the end, left him so alone.

Indeed, in his last week in the White House in January 1953, he was as friendless as few have ever been there. How poignantly this was so may be seen in a single anecdote. In respect for this man who had mastered so much that was timelessly vital, and had floundered in so much that was trivial and evanescent, I sent to President Truman a note saying that one unimportant observer with no political connections whatever and no partisan interest of any kind was convinced that history would put aright what contemporary accounts had altogether missed. How lonely he was, indeed! For this single letter of approval was so rare, in a house that stood then as now at the vital center of all the Western world's high interests, that it was read out at the President's last staff conference before he turned it all—the passing glories and the unending burdens—over to his successor, Dwight D. Eisenhower.

For these last hours in the Presidency dreadfully illustrated that power of the sustained stereotype, of the semantical and reiterative smear removed from all reality, to besmirch able men and wise policies which is held by the howling extremes of Right and Left when for totally different reasons they make common cause.

For Truman was brought down at last to what amounted to contemporary repudiation by a coalition of ultraconservative Republicans and ultraliberal Democrats who were not even conscious of how welded together they were. The first half of this frenetically irrational coalition sought his destruction because he would never carry sensible resistance to Communist expansionism to the point of madness—as, for illustration, the madness of attempting to wrest mainland China from the grip of the immovably entrenched Communists.

The second half of the coalition, the ultraliberals, set out almost from the opening of his administration to work his defeat and discredit precisely because he *was* resolute in rational resistance, beginning with his Greece-Turkey policy and ending with his courage and fortitude in Korea. They began a flanking attack upon him the moment he put his Truman Doctrine into play, and for this evolving cabal they found a willing, if naïvely innocent, human implement in Henry A. Wallace. Wallace had been Roosevelt's Vice-President, of course, until at the 1944 wartime Democratic Convention he had been dumped for reasons already given. Like James F. Byrnes on the Democratic right wing, Wallace on the left entered the Truman Cabinet in 1945 with little respect and even less love for his new chief. He found it impossible either to support the new President's sensibly anti-Communist policies or to remain publicly loyal to him. So, again like Byrnes, he was at length discharged by Truman from the Cabinet, and he went off to brood upon measures for vindication and, in his inflexibly Calvinist way, also for personal revenge.

The opportunity, as Wallace saw it, was not late in coming. When the Democratic National Convention met in 1948 in Philadelphia, Truman's essential position, both in the country and in his party, was seemingly one of rarely paralleled weakness, considering that he still held the bastion of the White House. Far-liberal Democrats, some inside and some outside the splinter organization called Americans for Democratic Action, began to prepare a Putsch against him in the hope of denying him renomination. The basic political insight they showed may be indicated by the fact that their preferred alternative was a man named General Dwight D. Eisenhower.

The ultraliberals' bill of particulars against Truman was complex, one of its items being, of course, that under his leadership the Democrats had lost control of Congress in Rayburn's "beefsteak election" of 1946. But in back of it all was a puerile distaste for Truman personally. Now, these anti-Truman Democrats were by no means themselves Communists, nor was Henry Wallace, who in the end became the symbol of leftist rebellion against the Truman administration. They were simply men who shrank from the use of force in international affairs, believing overmuch in the usefulness of "negotiations" with armed international aggressors, as later they were to believe overmuch in the same process as to the Communist invaders of South Vietnam.

The convention at Philadelphia thus met in an atmosphere of deep gloom and of deep divisions within the Democratic party. So low was Truman's estate that though he was only President of the United States of America, he was kept waiting for hours upon a rusty iron staircase outside the convention hall while the delegates pondered his fate. At last, as was inevitable, he was renominated. But only the shouting exertions of his old friend Senator Alben Barkley of Kentucky, who in a keynote speech summoned the partisans to draw together and to have faith where there was so little faith to be discerned, were able to keep Philadelphia from sounding like a wake for a lost man and lost cause.

Truman—of whom an admirer at the time observed in a Philadelphia bar that "anyhow the little guy has got moxie"—sallied forth from the convention with undiminished combat spirit and with aggression in his heart only for the wicked Republicans. Those defecting comrades who had so lately sought to smash him he genuinely forgave; he rallied his tattered and highly reluctant Democratic troops as once he had rallied his decimated artillery battery in France.

Wallace and the more extreme among the apostate

Democrats would not and could not accept the Philadelphia convention's verdict. They went off into the night —along with a good many Dixiecrat delegates in revolt against the convention's civil rights plank—and in due course nominated Henry Agard Wallace as a third-party candidate for President on a platform highly pleasing to the violent left—not excluding the Communist left— which had seen in the honorable but hopelessly soft Wallace a vehicle of opportunity.

All this, it might be thought, had filled Truman's plate pretty well; but the end was not yet. For the far-right wing of the Democrats saw an opportunity of its own; and so chose a fourth-party and Dixiecrat candidate called Strom Thurmond of South Carolina. So it fell out that Harry Truman's stewardship of the Democratic party had met catastrophic failure. Beleaguered by ultraconservatives on his right and by ultraliberals on his left, he had remaining only his center. And with this, as a famous French general had observed of his own situation in the First World War, he set out not to defend but to attack.

Matters for Truman were meanwhile far from improved by the choice by the Republican National Convention of 1948 of Governor Thomas E. Dewey of New York, who had unsuccessfully challenged Franklin D. Roosevelt in 1944 and might well have won but for the fact that a war was on and the people felt a traditional disinclination to change horses in the middle of the stream.

The ensuing campaign in the fall pitted a man who was both a great President and a poor politician against seemingly overwhelming and invincible Republican forces who were being given important aid and comfort from turncoat Democrats. All the pollsters and practically everybody else entitled to claim political expertise read the funeral lines over Harry Truman's dead body very early in the game. But he won; not, sadly, for his qualities as President but because of Republican mistakes which had alienated both the Middlewestern farmers and the emerging Negro voters and because of the irrepressible campaign arrogance of Thomas Dewey, a man of great administrative gifts and patriotism but of an inner political ruthlessness that seeped through in the end to the voters. And yet, 1948 victory or not, the seeds of ultimate defeat for Harry Truman had all the same been sown. He returned to office with a mandate, to be sure, but he returned as well with the implacable hostility of both the far right and the far left. All the grand and brave decisions he had made on *the* one issue of the time, that of foreign policy, would forever honor him, but would never save him from this insoluble contemporary reality. Here was a man who had calmly taken the frightful decision to drop the first atomic bomb—a decision he took because the alternative, he had been advised by Secretary of War Stimson, would be to risk half a million American casualties in storming the home island of Japan at a time when the United States was still counting its melancholy casualties from the war in Europe.

Here was a man who quietly, without self-pity, without attempts at self-justification, had lived with that frightful decision and had, to boot, made so many more of fateful grandeur. He had created the North Atlantic

66

Treaty, arming it as a great shield to all the Western world, and he had thus calmly and resolutely for the first time committed American troops for indefinite duty overseas in a time of nominal peace. He had broken the Soviet blockade of isolated Berlin, sending American supply aircraft ceaselessly into and out of that beleaguered city to save its life and to maintain there the Western position, which the Russians to this day still seek to compromise and to break. Here, as always, too, he had rejected the unwise and inadmissibly dangerous alternative that had been pressed upon him—frontal ground assaults right through the encircling Russian troop line, which might well have opened the Third World War.

And he had gone into South Korea to repel, at appalling cost and with great valor, the first clear Communist challenge to collective security since he had long ago checked another of that ilk along the Mediterranean. Again, in Korea, too, he had refused jingoistic counsel to "go all out"; for going all out might well have not only involved him massively with the Red Chinese but also would surely have weakened the NATO shield which he had so patiently raised over Europe.

For his pains in Korea what was his payment? It was a rising clamor at home, as the casualty lists lengthened, that he was at once too soft on Communism and too hard. The simplists from right and left now got him at last by the throat; and while he brought salvation to South Korea he brought contumely upon himself. The long indictments of him did not stop there. For he became a victim, too, of Senator Joseph R. McCarthy, that professional Communist-hunter who for three years all but destroyed effective government in this country by endless and distorted attacks upon the integrity of government itself, and notably upon the integrity of Harry Truman. So, the damage was done; the last clouds now gathered about Harry Truman.

For the President who had summarily broken and recalled an idolized field commander in Korea, General Douglas MacArthur, for insubordinate attempts to broaden the war beyond its prudent scope, now found himself pictured as really against a victory in that war. There it stood, then, "Communism, Cronyism, Corruption, Korea." This became the litany against Harry Truman in the early fifties, and the truth was lost amid the debris of destructive slogans.

As the year 1952 and his first elected Presidential term drew jointly toward their close, all the forces of the Irresponsibles—the men alike of good and ill intention united only by their determination to bring down this tired and unarticulate gallant leader—closed in about him. In the New Hampshire Democratic primary of March, which is traditionally the first to be held in the nation and thus holds a propaganda power a hundred times its meaning in logical terms, the name of Harry S. Truman trailed that of a highly publicity-conscious Senator from Tennessee called Estes Kefauver. Kefauver was by no means a bad man; only a limited, demagogic man wholly uncomprehending of the majesty and the misery of the Presidential office. To speak of him as a successor to Harry Truman was in fact to speak a towering nonsense; but here unreason won not the first of its victories. And in the meantime Truman's Republican opposition was everywhere asking voters the question, by way of automobile bumper stickers and in the press and radio, "Had enough?"

Whether the voters themselves, granted a more rational public climate, had truly had enough of Truman will never be known by history. For Harry Truman himself had had enough; and so on March 29 he quietly announced that he would not run again. Thus it was that an incredible era, an era of the most brilliant of world statesmanship accompanied step by step by a failing domestic and party leadership, ended at last with never a bang but never a whimper.

Truman, on his last day in the White House, decorously carried out his full duty as departing host to his successor, Dwight D. Eisenhower, and gravely prepared to walk, repeat *walk*, to the station with Mrs. Truman to take a train to Missouri and so to leave Washington forever without fuss and in poignantly simple dignity. He had thought that all the White House limousines would be required by the people of the new regime until old friends persuaded him that there would really be no pushy impropriety in his making one last use of a government vehicle.

Long ago, toward the very beginning, he had once observed, "There are probably a million people in this country who could do the Presidential job better than I can; but I've got the job and I am going to do the very best I can."

It was an estimate honestly meant, but among those who would never agree with it was a man who had come to scoff inside himself at Harry S. Truman but had remained to praise. For among the memories that Truman took back on the train to Independence with him was of a night on the Presidential yacht *Williamsburg* when for the last time he was in any intimate sense the host to the British Prime Minister. They sat, these two old warriors, in the ward room, alone save for Roger Tubby, who was then the President's press secretary. Churchill, mellowed by brandy and full of the remembrance of the days of danger and decision he had shared with his friend, leaned across the dining table and paid to him the ultimate accolade. There was no tape recorder there and Tubby cannot now recollect the Prime Minister's precise text. But it came to this: "Mr. President, you more than any man, now alive or now dead, have saved the Western world and all its values as we have known them."

• • •

BOOK THREE

Robert A. Taft

• • •

Robert A. Taft is long dead now, but of this oddly apolitical politician, this shy, lonely and prickly introvert in an extravert's profession and world, a rare thing, indeed, may be said. The old aphorism has it that a statesman is only a dead politician; in Taft's case the interposition of death was not required to transform him, either in popular legend or in fact, from the one to the other. He was a statesman in his own time, and so accepted.

His long march through the field of public affairs—a bald, pale, cantankerous pilgrim who seemed always to dislike too many and too much but whose only real enemies were cant and demagoguery and intellectual fakery —led him to the very doors of the Presidency but never quite through them.

He earned it, but he never received it; for the quality of paradox that is one of the most pervasive realities of American politics was never kind to Robert Alphonso Taft. Still, in a sense his career was enriched by defeat as it might never have been had he been victorious in his last and nearest challenge for the Presidential office, in 1952. For the long and short of it is that to the rival who denied the nomination to him, General Dwight D. Eisenhower, Taft became, briefly but memorably, a kind of Prime Minister to another's republican monarchy. In the early months of the Eisenhower administration, which opened in 1953, there was, of course, no question that the final power rightly rested in the hands of the new President. But there was the most genuine question as to whether some of the President's most momentous decisions had not in fact originated in the extraordinary mind of Senator Robert Taft of Ohio. Waggish critics said that it was "the best eighteenth-century mind in the Senate," but this was a quip in which humor was allowed to overturn truth, as many another political mot has done and will do.

For the truth is that the Eisenhower administration was guided by Robert Taft with a skill and a quiet, self-sacrificing gallantry which has had no other exact example in the life of this republic and which was no less important for having been so subtly offered and so little known beyond the inner councils of the American government. The Taft who had been defeated at the 1952 Republican National Convention by General Eisenhower—a newcomer to politics and the symbol of the national mood "It's Time for a Change"—made a rare sort of accommodation with his late adversary. It was scarcely less magnanimous in political terms than was Robert E. Lee's in military terms when he bowed in defeat to U.S. Grant at Appomattox Courthouse. Each in the end, Lee in Virginia and Taft in Washington nearly a century later, was seized by the ultimate conviction of national duty. And both responded, with no further thought of private ambition, no further malice toward victors who had used them hard while the guns were still going, no further concern for any personal tomorrow.

The year 1952 was one of a twilight turning in American politics. It ended twenty years of Democratic domination of public affairs from the White House, first under Franklin D. Roosevelt and then under Harry S. Truman. It also brought revolutionary changes in the locus of power within the Republican party, substantially removing that locus from the traditional Republican heartland in the Middle West to the Eastern seaboard, and in the process putting the orthodox Republicans on a very thin diet indeed. The vehicle for these convulsions was General Dwight D. Eisenhower; the victim was Senator Robert Taft.

When the Republicans had seized control of Congress from the Truman Democrats in 1946 they had had in Robert Taft a new leader ready at hand and eminently suitable within a political party that still prized *suitability* as it had long prized the tradition that leadership really ought to go only to the right people. Taft was incomparably of the right people. His father, the somewhat Falstaffian William Howard Taft, whose home ground was in Ohio but who was nevertheless anything but an outlander to the board rooms of New York and Boston, had been both a President and a Chief Justice of the United States. Robert Taft was both his legal and his spiritual heir. Ordained to party headship, he was enough like his father in surface matters—a believer in the obvious right of the Republican party to rule, a faithful communicant of the Alexander Hamiltonian creed that government was at last the proper business of the rich and well-born—to hide decently the vast real differences between the elder and the younger Tafts.

When, therefore, the Eightieth—and Republican—Congress assembled in January 1947, Robert Taft became in that moment the intellectual and moral leader of not only one but rather both of its houses. And at the same moment he became "Mister Republican." He had undeniably helped to prepare the Republican Congressional victories in the autumn of 1946, and even more significantly he was the one national Republican figure aptly and truly mirroring the party's real differences with President Harry Truman and with the Democratic party in general.

From his seat in the Senate—which characteristically was never in the front row, for as a high political commander he would have shuddered at the very notion that a General of the Armies should take so vulgar a course as to put himself obviously and melodramatically at the physical head of his troops—Taft set off to direct a restoration of the Republican party to its place of proper primacy.

His view of the Roosevelt and Truman years had been most gloomy. It was not so much that they had changed so much and so many in American life. He never supposed (though millions of Americans never understood this) that change was bad in itself. Nor did he ever consider that the ways of tradition, either in government or in personal affairs, were sacred or unalterable. The core of his conviction was that the immense changes he had seen had been made imprudently, by men who were themselves imprudent, and that on the whole they had unfairly altered the individual citizen's relationship to the federal power.

He was not, in fact, a "rugged individualist" in the sense that President Herbert Hoover had been misunderstood by most of the population to be during the grim days of the Great Depression of the thirties. He did not, that is to say, believe that the only good American was a fellow eternally suspicious of *all* government and solely dedicated to getting himself forward at the expense, if need be, of any and all others.

No. Taft's quarrel with the Roosevelt-Truman Democrats was actually more philosophical than political in ordinary terms; though, again, the Republican rank and file, including many of his own most passionate partisan followers, never grasped this, either. He thought, in brief, that for two decades the Democrats, in their great hurry to relieve human need, had introduced a concept of public welfarism so oversimplified as to take into too little account the more fundamental concepts of personal responsibility and inalienable private rights. He thought, too, that there had been altogether too much easy sloganeering in a social revolution to which he was not in fact altogether hostile in principle.

So much was this the case, to be sure, that he became habitually antislogan and particularly hostile to such slogans as had been natural to a reformist era.

Thus, for illustration, when at the beginning of the

Eisenhower administration in 1953 it was proposed to create a new Cabinet department dedicated by definition to social change, Taft readily assisted the necessary legislative enabling acts, but, with rare profanity, balked at its recommended title: "The Department of Welfare." So the administration bowed, as so often it would bow again to Senator Robert Taft, and accepted the alternative designation now in use: "The Department of Health, Education and Welfare."

"Health" and "Education" were to Taft respectable words, simple and plain. Above all, they were not stained by that reformist rhetoric, that earnest social-worker patois, which to Taft consisted not so much of fighting words as of words whose regrettable inexactitude and whose deplorably liberal aroma were rather like the odor of cathedral candles to an atheist compelled to attend a funeral mass for a friend.

But, and far more important, of course, Taft was motivated, too, by a genuine interest in promoting health and education above all other things and was not willing to see these matters take second place behind a far less definable thing called welfare.

Here, in short, was a very uncommon man indeed. He was an aristocrat (by common American standards of birth and means and social standing) who never really knew he was and in any case could not have cared less. He was, in action, a most faithful partisan to whom the ordinary drill of partisanship was nevertheless a dreadful bore, and the inevitable hand-shaking an act to be severely rationed and undertaken at all only with a candid displeasure that was highly disconcerting to those who wished only the best for his future. Once, for example, when he was seeking the Presidential nomination of 1952, this writer was talking to the Senator off the Senate floor about one of those affairs that truly engaged his attention—a legislative bill. Representative Clarence Brown of Ohio, an old and matchlessly constant figure in the Taft political apparatus, interrupted to bring urgent political intelligence having to do with the coming Republican National Convention. Taft heard him out with unconcealed impatience and sent him on his way with this testy comment to me, right in Brown's ear: "Sorry about this interruption; a fellow in politics has got to put up sometimes with this kind of thing. Now, about this bill . . ."

Again, he was widely seen as stuffily humorless, an estimate promoted by his rarely relieved preoccupation with the purely impersonal in public issues and in politics. But his genuine sense of humor was both subtle and bleak. It was ironically detached, a long way from the belly laugh and from those smoking-room jollities from which all his life he recoiled, metaphorically a man in a high starched collar who could not have been more spiritually alone among the barbecue pits and the country club Saturday nights of his home town of Cincinnati. Still, to those who knew him well (and very few, even among his oldest associates, ever really knew him at all) his sense of the ridiculous was as acute as was his sense of perspective. He never told a joke, as such, but an ironic gaiety could flash from him as from few other politicians of his rank and stature.

For an example, his wife, Martha, was a far more crustily regular Middlewestern Republican than even he ever thought to be and her sturdily simple divisions of sheep and goats gave him an enormous private and affectionate amusement. Upon the onset of the Second World War Martha Taft was proudly and typically an Ohio isolationist, and more deeply suspicious both of British guile and of the current dynasty of the rival Roosevelt house, Franklin D., than ever Taft had been. The rector of the Episcopal Church ordinarily attended by Mr. and Mrs. Taft, the first attending in a kind of absent-minded habit and the second with true zeal, was a strong prowar man and, specifically, an earnest advocate of American intervention against Hitler.

Martha Taft found his attitude intolerable and quietly left the Episcopal Church as a whole. Taft himself never referred to this episode until, many years later, I idly inquired of him about his and her religious connections. "Martha, you know, quit the Episcopal Church way back," he remarked.

"What church does she have now?"

Taft smiled—an oddly striking smile, since it was so rarely in evidence—and replied, "Really don't know; think she's still shopping around for another one."

This quality of personal detachment was from beginning to end a factor in his political career; a largely harmful one to him, since it involved a collateral unwillingness to explain himself in any detail on any occasion. Yet it permitted him to maintain an extraordinary private objectivity rarely seen in public life, just as it made him almost wholly unpredictable in personal terms. A friend once wrote a magazine article which was essentially critical of the Senator, and he was in consequence a bit doubtful about the reception he would receive when next they met. His concern was unnecessary. For Taft, far from bridling at the criticism, wholly ignored the substance of the article to speak with animation of its style. "Almost a literary touch there," he said. "Don't see much of that in popular journalism."

Again, when he lost his temper (and this he did on frequent occasions) he did not lose it as most men would. He never resented attacks upon him or his policies when he believed them to have been made ably and without personal malice. But he could respond with incandescent anger to the most favorable critiques, even when they faithfully supported some current purpose of his, when he considered them poorly argued or put in poor English. "Puerile!" he would snap, "simply puerile."

No politician known to me ever suffered less gladly persons he believed to be fools or ideas he believed to be foolish. Toward such men and such ideas he turned a face of glacial displeasure, and as it happened the victims in both categories were very often his own fellow Republicans in the Senate. When he heard a colleague make what he thought to be a silly point or a silly speech he would glare about with open contempt. And he was capable, on rare occasions, of uttering loud asides to the offender which could be heard all over the Senate: "For Heaven's sake, sit down." He never accepted the titular floor leadership of his party, preferring to sit aloofly back as chairman of its Policy Committee, on the entirely unhidden theory that *he* would make the policy and let some other and lesser fellow carry it on from there. A lawyer by training, he was very much like the solicitor in England who takes general charge of the defense but leaves it to the barrister to get down into the sweaty arena of appealing to the jury.

Nevertheless, he made party strategy as did no other Republican, whatever his office, in his time. And his frequent trespasses—open impatience with slower minds, or open displeasure with "foolishness"—were forgiven him as they would never have been forgiven another. For no sensible man, whether party friend or foe, could long doubt that Taft's essential purposes were large purposes and, at the most, only collaterally directed to the nurture and promotion of Robert A. Taft personally.

So it was that he exercised an extraordinary party headship. If it was far more harshly patriarchial than benevolently avuncular, it had in it, nevertheless, the sort of cool kindness toward partisan colleagues that really counted. For while he never for a moment held their hands in sympathy, and almost never patted a back in approval, he did something incomparably more useful for them. He was, when they were in electoral trouble, the shepherd among the sheep; he made a party record that both embraced them all and protected them all. In a word, he did for years a good deal of the genuinely creative thinking for the whole Republican tribe.

When he himself stood, rarely, in the Senate to carry the Republican brief, he did so without a shadow of eloquence but with power all the same. He was, in voice, flat, nasal; and what he lacked in emotional appeal—which was very much—he more than compensated for by his command of the facts. He made his case like a professor of mathematics laying down an indisputable equation, or like a carpenter hammering down nails. The artifices of debate he scorned, because, when it came to the showdown, few in the Senate in either party could contest with him, mind to mind.

This, then, was the kind of mind and man who set off in the Eightieth Congress to redeem his party's fortunes and, not least, to harass the far more humble former Senate colleague who was now down at the White House, Harry Truman. Characteristically, Taft's immediate concerns zeroed in upon domestic matters; given his view of what was wrong with the Democrats, this had to be the priority.

What was singly most wrong, as he saw it, was a dangerous and growing imbalance of power between labor and management which had arisen under Franklin Roosevelt's Wagner Act, a law that had slowly given the labor unions an undue strength in the running economic contest with business. Taft, therefore, made ready for what would turn out to be his magnum opus—and it was uniquely apropos that this should be so, since the issue he had seized was both highly important and inescapably dull to a country still full of the hot, red memories of a global war.

He opened a campaign fundamentally to revise the labor law of the nation, and it would all end at last in the Taft-Hartley Act. The substance of this bill, as it was ultimately refined and passed and then repassed over President Truman's veto, was to restore the labor-management power balance to something approaching stable equilibrium, to cut down somewhat on labor's primacy.

But the road between the beginning and the end ran long and confused, and it provided a climactic test of Robert Taft's high political capacity and basic devotion to objective national interest—interest transcending party and ideology. Most of his Republican colleagues had celebrated their return to Congressional power in a mood both unduly vengeful and resting upon the most doubtful assumptions. They believed that the elections of 1946 had signaled a wide and unqualified popular revulsion from the Democratic party as such, and not, as was the fact of the case, simply a transitory spasm of irritation against things as things then were. The voters had repudiated a certain number of Democratic Congressmen; they had not repudiated the essential history of either the Roosevelt or Truman eras, as was later to be altogether too plainly shown.

And as to the first point, the view of the Republican Congressional consensus that the people had given them a mandate not merely to rule but also to seek revenge was to give Taft about as much trouble with his party colleagues as he would ever meet from his overt and traditional Democratic opposition. He never sought revenge for revenge's sake. Where most of his fellow partisans interpreted the election to mean that the public wanted to "get tough with labor," Taft's wiser estimate was simply that the public instead wanted only a more sensible industrial power balance by checking labor but not a destruction of the unions.

Thus, Taft's colleague in the Taft-Hartley Act from the side of the House of Representatives, Representative

Fred Hartley of New Jersey, set out to write a bill against labor so plainly and so harshly punitive as utterly to enrage the labor unions and also deeply to annoy Taft. The House and part of the Senate were still in fury at memories of irresponsible strikes during wartime in essential industries and were of a mood simply to hit out wildly at all unions. Of this mood Hartley was an apt human embodiment.

Taft, to the contrary, was here—as nearly always—concerned not with emotional reactions but only with rational and workable reform. Though he had, God knows, little reason to love Labor with a capital "L," since that kind of Labor had all his life earnestly sought the vitals of Robert Taft, he had no smallest intention to allow the loud evangelism of the House to overcome that spirit of cool reason in which, again nearly always, he himself operated.

The most powerful of the labor leaders, on their side, instantly took up an adamant and howling position against any and all change in the law and, in consequence, from the onset cried out that what Taft was about was a "slave labor" enactment. Taft took all this nonsense from the left with a tolerant scorn, and characteristically turned his main efforts to subtly beating his supposed ally, Representative Hartley, over the head to indoctrinate him with the high necessity to produce at length a sensible and not a mere screed of an enactment.

To put the thing with unkind candor, Hartley was just short of the openly biddable creature of the ultraconservative part of industrial management; Taft was, as always, the creature of nobody but Taft. And far from naïve as he surely was, he was himself so removed from the grosser improprieties of politics that he never really grasped the associations with big campaign contributors that were all but visible around the person and the motives of the cheerfully maneuverable and pedestrian Hartley.

This quality of unawareness, this instinctive rejection of the mere possibility that men holding high elective office *under the Republicans* could be open to crude pressures, was both an endearing and a frustrating factor in Taft's make-up. Thus, when, in the late forties and early fifties Joseph R. McCarthy of Wisconsin was engaged in a cruel and fraudulent attack upon alleged Communists within the State Department, Taft simply could not believe that a Senator of the United States would habitually make the grave accusations that McCarthy was making without honest proof and without personally disinterested purposes. The tragic consequence was that Taft, the greatest Congressional Republican in his or in any other era, allowed McCarthy to run loose without rebuke, not from the slightest lack of decency but simply because the world of Robert Taft never, never knew the world of the Joseph McCarthys.

Retrospective speculation is always interesting academically—and is usually also dangerous. Still, it is certain that had Taft known what was easily discernible to others who were both more perceptive men and lesser men, the McCarthy era would have ended long before it did in fact end with an act of Senate condemnation that was arranged not by other Republicans, as it really should have been, but rather by the then Senate Democratic leader, Lyndon B. Johnson.

86

Still, if awareness of the existence of evil was never one of Taft's strong points—in part because temperamentally he recoiled from any mixing of moral judgments with political actions—the application of pure reason to political issues was his strong suit. It was through this application that he was at length able to bring out of the Republican Eightieth Congress a labor-management act so truly fair to both parties that it has stood basically unaltered in all the years since.

It was, of course, an achievement that was also immensely significant in purely political terms, but it was only one highlight of this strange man's contributions to the legislative history of this country.

For he fought for such concepts as Federal housing and Federal aid to education in the days when the former was otherwise an almost exclusively Democratic political preserve and the latter was still being very cautiously approached even by liberal Democrats.

This unceasing preoccupation with issues that were by definition liberal, and in fact at that time very liberal indeed, by the untitled conservative leader of the United States troubled Taft's admirers, touched his critics against their will with reluctant admiration—and highly amused Taft. I once asked him how he, of all men, could support Federal aid to education. "Why not?" he replied. "Of course, there is an undeniable touch of plain socialism in all this, but then public education is essentially socialist in meaning anyhow, isn't it?"

It was more or less his attitude also toward public housing, a matter upon which he very often joined liberal Democrats—while they looked at him in wry, unbelieving wonderment, and he looked at them with much the expression of a banker finding himself unaccountably visiting a settlement house with, say, a Tammany district leader. The point here was that Taft truly, if rather inarticulately, believed in a good deal of Federal welfarism but in behalf of, and solely in behalf of, those persons he considered in his heart to be the irresponsibles. These, to him, were the children. If an adult got himself into economic trouble Taft's general view was that, well, it must be his own fault. But if a child had no decent place in which to live, no decent prospect of a fair education, he had a resolute sympathizer in Taft of Ohio —the same Taft who could scarcely have conceived of sending his own children to any place outside the ivied halls of private education.

This ambivalence was consistently expressed at great political cost to Taft personally. It never earned him an ounce of gratitude from the liberal Republicans. If it never brought him the actual condemnation of the conservatives, it always shook them up a bit—and always at the wrong time, as when a party convention was about to meet.

Most of all, however, the fact that he never became President of the United States, and was never even nominated for that office, had to do with his attitudes on foreign policy. For years he was generally put down as a kind of isolationist—another simplistic stereotype that seems fated to dog the Responsibles of our history— though he never was really that at all.

The circumstances of his time, to be sure, identified him as primarily concerned with, and primarily a leader of, the domestic issues. But his foreign concerns were always high and not by any means always lacking in perceptiveness.

All the same, fresh from his magnificent record of party leadership in the Eightieth Congress, he went to his last, and his climactic, party nominating convention in 1952 as a man who had demonstrably earned the nomination on the tests of experience and party achievement but nevertheless as a man destined to lose.

In a subtle but powerful way this very model of the proper Republican had alienated the very board rooms that were his natural heritage. For Eastern Republicanism wanted not only the fresh, handsome face that was General Dwight D. Eisenhower's but also was skeptical, in foreign matters, of the tired, homely face that was Taft's. He himself had spent a good deal of time in attacking the Truman administration's foreign policies, especially NATO. Truman and Dean Acheson had put this through the Senate with the decisive assistance of board-room men and of Senator Arthur Vandenberg of Michigan, who had been a total isolationist during the Second World War but had suffered a great Paulist conversion to internationalism upon the onset of the peace.

Taft, moreover, had shown lively sympathy with General of the Army Douglas MacArthur, whom Truman had recalled from his Korean command for contumacious designs to go over the head of the White House itself and thus greatly to widen the war. And, to put a cap upon it all, Taft had fallen in with an articulate Big Bomber minority in this country, which though not quite prepared to endorse an outright preventive war against Red China was plainly ready to take up a policy of going to the very brink of it to arrest the momentum of Communist expansionism in Asia.

Taft's position thus became oversimplified into one of anti-Europe and pro-Asia; and he himself did not help matters by a persistent unwillingness to explain himself in detail. He had the aristocrat's distaste for self-justification, compounded by a stubborn belief that other people were more perceptive than most other people ever were.

The ironic truth is that the whole general thrust of his foreign policy views was anything but isolationist and was in fact very forward-looking in some ways. He understood, for example, the real nature of the developing Free World–Communist collision in Asia a good deal ahead of time. At bottom, his philosophy shrank from any American strategy dependent mainly upon the use of ground forces. And while this led him in those old days to question NATO and the commitment to it of American troops, it was not fair—though it was very easy—simply to write him off as a politician who didn't want to do much to protect Europe.

The fact is, too, that while he fought ratification of the NATO treaty with great determination (in the process brushing abrasively against a future Secretary of State called John Foster Dulles), one thing can never be taken from his record. This is that almost alone among the Senators of that time he insisted upon clearly stating that NATO was not going to be some mere vague brotherly association of Atlantic powers but rather the first military alliance ever entered upon by this nation in a time of formal peace. In a word, his very attacks upon the treaty gave it far more dignity than did the various defenses of it which were made by men—including the then Senator Dulles—whose desire to see it ratified led them into understating the grandeur, and the reality, of its grave pledges of one for all and all for one.

So it was that Taft was planning his supreme effort for the Presidential nomination in the spring of 1952 while doing his very best to make it difficult for himself, both by adopting positions outside the contemporary foreign-policy mainstream and by characteristically allowing them to be unintentionally misrepresented by a Washington press corps which he habitually handled with a majestically chill tactlessness.

Sitting one day in a visitors' room just off the Senate floor, he discussed his prospects with a friend. Referring to the fact that he would clearly go to the convention with far more pledged delegates in hand than would General Eisenhower, he added, in the most offhand way, a bleak postscript: "Still, all this doesn't mean that I am in."

"But why not?" he was asked.

"Well," he said, "it sounds strange for me of all people to be hitting at 'Wall Street,' but the fact is that Eisenhower has got something I haven't got. Yes, the rich will support me—but the very, very rich will support him." It was, in other words, already dimly apparent to him that he had broken dangerously with what was later to be called the Eastern Republican Establishment. The Establishment did not really trust him on foreign policy and even more preferred the sheer glamour attached to the name of Dwight Eisenhower, the conqueror, for the record, of Adolf Hitler.

Moreover, General Douglas MacArthur, a hero indeed to many in this country in the afterlight of his emotional response to Harry Truman's decision to break him, seemed then himself a potential figure of power for the Republican Convention. This aspect of the matter, however, the possibility that MacArthur, too, might be a conventional rival, bothered Taft not at all. "Nonsense! Nonsense!" he said in his flat Ohio voice. "Who the devil is going to prefer MacArthur's fire to my frying pan?" In this estimate, he was quite right. MacArthur's star sank before the convention was two days old, and the contest became strictly one between Robert A. Taft and Dwight D. Eisenhower.

Taft was the ordained Old Guardist, though he never was truly an Old Guarder. Eisenhower was the New Hope, though at the time nobody really knew whether he was at heart a Republican or a Democrat. Taft had far more of the delegate votes; Eisenhower had the matchless assets of the favor of the vast bulk of the opinion-making apparatus of the country, plus the wide assumption that he could win in November and that Taft could not. And even more important, as it turned out, Eisenhower had the great boon of the ineptitude of Taft's cadre of *really* Old Guard advisers, the American Bourbons, of whom it could truly be said that they never learned anything and forgot everything.

In the normal preconvention maneuvering the Taft people had blotted their copybook in Texas, where erstwhile Democrats had rushed into the Republican primaries to seek to smash Taft and to promote Eisenhower. The net of it was that the Taft apparatus clearly had won the Texas delegation by the old rules—and if one chose to define the Texas delegation as properly made up only of genuine Republicans. But the Eisenhower apparatus had won the delegation if one chose to accept crypto-Democrats as its proper members.

Eisenhower's managers—Thomas E. Dewey of New York and Henry Cabot Lodge of Massachusetts—brilliantly exploited all this confusion by raising a vast "moral issue" against Taft, claiming that he, or rather his people, had tried to "steal" the Texas delegation. Taft himself watched all this with absolute amazement. Unalterably candid himself, he knew perfectly well that the Taft people in Texas had operated within the unwritten rules of the game, had done nothing by way of delegate snatching that the other side had not done, too.

His attitude at the convention was an unforgettable study in fastidious uncomprehension. The Eisenhower people were running what they called "a crusade," and crusades were as foreign to both the public personality and the private taste of Taft as would have been, say, a public confession of sins at a revival meeting in the canebrakes. Watching the development of the "great moral issue" against him, Taft was a man in embarrassed and total exasperation. An utterly illogical but nevertheless powerful factor had been brought into play against him, and for a critically long time he found it quite impossible to believe that sensible men—and sensible *Republican* men at that—could possibly be long influenced by it at a convention which was supposed to nominate a perfectly logical contender for the Presidency.

As he glumly eyed the carefully arranged "spontaneous parades" of delegates carrying banners proclaiming that Commandment which says "Thou Shalt Not Steal," and parades also carefully arranged by the Dewey-Lodge field captains for Eisenhower to occur under the brightest of the television lights, Taft was both too late in grasping the nature of his peril and too blunt in dealing with it when at length the peril became clear even to him. Instead of mounting a counterpropaganda campaign proclaiming his tormentors to be mere screeching evangelists, as any other politician in his position would surely have done, he simply suggested at last that, very well, he would *share* the Texas delegates with the Eisenhower forces. Now, of course, they had him truly where they had wanted him. For the very compromise which he had proposed, upon the advice of campaign associates, whose devotion to him was exceeded only by their capacity to put their worst foot forward at the worst possible time in his behalf, amounted to a confession that there had, indeed, been hanky-panky in Texas by the Taft forces.

The consequence was a sudden convention breakthrough by the Eisenhower people, and the man who had gone there with far the greater power in real terms became overwhelmed on the convention floor by the exploitation of one of those mundane political factors which Robert Taft could never understand. This was the factor of "public relations." It was a case of a Goliath of immense ability on the great and substantive matters of public affairs overwhelmed by a David of no experience or record whatever upon such matters but a David who was, nevertheless, the beneficiary of a giant public relations campaign which was the very best that both money and honest pro-Eisenhower conviction could buy.

A strange parallel could be seen by perceptive onlookers at that convention. The Taft who was by common consent the absolute antithesis of Harry Truman shared with his old bête noire both a singular capacity for national leadership in its high and indispensable forms and a singular weakness for routine politics in its far lower but also quite indispensable forms. Whether either man ever understood his odd community of interest with the other is, of course, never to be known. It is, however, rationally possible to take the view that this was the case. For when, later on, Taft was literally dying on his feet in the Senate and the retiring President Harry S. Truman was paying a last, sentimental call to that body, he went directly to the desk of Robert Taft and put out his hand with a warmth shown to no other man on that day.

There they stood, Taft on crutches, full of the unacknowledged pain of a raging bone cancer, and Truman still strong and well. They looked at each other with quiet smiles, Truman in an openly emotional attitude and Taft indomitably cool and determinedly offhand in a way that fooled nobody at all. It was a memorably touching unexpressed farewell between two great Responsibles whose contributions to the ultimate public interest could not in their own time save them from the easy popular repudiation that is so often the interim fate of the Responsibles until history comes at last to square accounts.

Taft left the 1952 Republican National Convention under one of the most bitter disappointments ever to befall

a truly qualified aspirant for the Presidential nomination. "Mister Republican" had been beaten by a rank
amateur, and not only beaten but also presented to the
country—this very model of decorum and prudence and
irreproachable public and private morality—as a kind of
political burglar who had besmirched the annals of convention struggles.

Still, to no one did he let his guard down; to no one
did he utter a word of anger or of anguish. And before
he departed, to go off to the Taft family summer place
in Murray Bay, Canada, to bind up in private wounds
that had been most publicly suffered, he wrote out a
memo to his lieutenants which amounted not to an argu-
ment but to an order from the chief.

Its sense was that whatever had happened to the Taft
campaign at the convention was the sole, the exclusive
and the not-to-be-debated responsibility of Robert Alphonso Taft. This was not merely an act of magnanimity, though it was all of that. It was an expression
of Taft's positive inability to allow lesser men to share
either his successes or his defeats. He could never stomach the passing of any buck downward, and this, indeed,
was always one of his qualities as a partisan antagonist
of the Democrats.

As a Senate Republican leader his attacks upon the
Truman administration, and retrospectively upon
Franklin Roosevelt's administration, had, Heaven
knows, never lacked for vigor in deep partisanship. He
had once, for example, unwisely justified these by the
snapped observation: "It is the business of the opposition
to oppose." But in all his oppositionism there was a sig-

nificant qualification. He went after the big game; he never shot at the tame rabbits. Thus, he invariably centered his fire—about the fall of China to the Communists, about any and every other issue that came to hand —upon a Harry Truman, a Roosevelt or, sometimes in a pinch, at some such technically secondary but still very powerful figure as a Secretary of State named Acheson, a fellow Yale man toward whom Taft took an attitude of pained disbelief.

But he was deeply annoyed when fellow Republicans lowered their gun sights to some relatively small bureaucrats below the senior Cabinet rank. Thus, though he had given to Joseph McCarthy a heartbreakingly free run, persisting in the belief that a Senator of the United States was by definition surely of the top rank in public responsibility, he later scornfully denounced attacks upon the loyalty of the career diplomat Charles Bohlen. The Eisenhower administration had unaccountably and, to Taft, simply incredibly, elevated Bohlen to high place in the State Department in the face of the undeniable fact that he had been at the Yalta Conference, which Taft always saw as a surrender to the Russians.

Bohlen's appointment had shaken Taft to the very core. And when truly right-wing, as opposed to Taftwing, Senate Republicans opened an assault upon the diplomat, Taft's initial instinct was to give it his approval. But this was before he was invited to serve upon an *ad hoc* Senate committee that went down to the Federal Bureau of Investigation to examine the dossier on Charles Bohlen.

Taft had a dozen times before this sat and listened

without complaint to other Senators' attacks upon men in the administration on the basis of "the FBI files." But this was the first time he himself had ever seen one. It was in itself a shaking experience. He returned to the Capitol in shocked disgust, for he had learned that a "raw" FBI file can and does carry not merely facts but also gossip and innuendo and sometimes mere malicious tittle-tattle. So he rose to the Senate floor to say that while the Bohlen appointment was repellent to him, in terms of impersonal public policy, Bohlen as a person had been noisomely maligned and should be confirmed forthwith—as Bohlen duly was.

Taft by this time, of course, had had some experience of his own of wild accusations; and no doubt most vividly in his memory were the cries of "Thou Shalt Not Steal" at the 1952 Republican Convention. This was an ordeal not easy to forget or to forgive; but Taft, upon due reflection, managed both forgetfulness and forgiveness toward General Eisenhower personally. Still, while he yet brooded at Murray Bay there were plain signals about the nation that the vast Taft Republican followership—and it was nothing less than this—would not accept the convention's decision, both because the Senator in the ordinary way had earned the nomination and because of the way it had been denied to him.

Taft was troubled by this; he rejected emotional approaches, whether against him or in his interest. He thus emerged from the Canadian silences to arrange a meeting with the new Republican Presidential candidate at Columbia University, where General Eisenhower had been president. This, the Conference of Morningside

Heights, resulted first in a Taft-Eisenhower cease-fire, then in an armistice and, at last, in an open alliance. Taft came out supporting General Eisenhower, and it was perfectly clear that while he had lost the convention he had gone far toward winning the mind of General Eisenhower upon some matters that were highly important.

Some called it "the Surrender (by Eisenhower) of Morningside Heights," though this was too strong altogether. But the new Presidential nominee had gone a long way to meet Taft's philosophic standards; and when the head man sent out his blessings upon Eisenhower the thus far sullen and inactive Taft troops moved up for the campaign in battle array for General Eisenhower. Not gladly did they move, but move they did. For Taft, unable as he had been to the end to engage the loyalties of a voting majority of the Republican Convention's voting delegates, beyond doubt had retained the operating headship of a Republican party that was far bigger than any convention's aggregate.

He had made no crude "deal" with Eisenhower at Columbia University, but it would very shortly be seen that his stamp upon the actions of an administration not yet elected would be highly legible.

For, from the moment of his inauguration in January 1953, President Eisenhower heeded Taft's advice to a degree and in ways and on issues far beyond the ordinary relationship between a President and a powerful Senator of his own party. It was advice tendered by Taft with the utmost in cool—not to say cold—protocol. He never pretended a personal fondness for the new President, just as he never for a moment betrayed the slightest touch of

99

friendship's opposite. His manner in his calls upon the President was as correctly impersonal as would have been that, say, of some foreign diplomat serving in Washington. But while his heart could never be engaged by the President, the best qualities of his mind and of his high political expertise were fully tapped at the White House. It was counsel extended in the somehow remote generosity which was one of Taft's oddest traits; it was counsel received by the President with respect and with a generosity of his own, since, after all, only one man at a time can be President.

Taft would return from his official calls at the White House to report on his missions to such Senatorial colleagues as he might choose with a wry aloofness of attitude, almost invariably referring to Eisenhower not as "the President," not as "Eisenhower," but simply as "he." It was plain that in discharging what he considered to be duties that were both obvious and less than inspiriting to him personally he was loyally doing his job but was often troubled at President Eisenhower's cheerful and sometimes quite extraordinary outer political innocence. Still, this consideration to the Senator was from first to last a minor matter. It was something to be briefly and bleakly smiled over, but nothing more than that. It did not lead Taft to suppose that the President had any fundamental incapacity for his job; it only led him to believe that the President needed the kind of assistance he, Taft, could give him.

Eisenhower, on his side, in spite of a deliberately and somehow appealingly amateurish approach and an open inclination to look upon many of the forms and trappings of politicking as mere tiresome "clackety-clack," was, in fact, an incomparably better politician than Taft ever thought—and in some respects a far better one than Taft himself. The President, in short, held the Senator in considerably higher esteem for his qualities in the profession of politics than Taft held the President in that regard.

Almost certainly, too, Eisenhower was more sensitively appreciative of Taft's magnificently contained disappointment than Taft himself ever knew. At all events, they made, for a critical time during the transition of power from one administration to another, a remarkably effective if also a remarkably arm's-length team. At first, of course, as was inevitable under the circumstances, there were a few rasping episodes. One of these involved the selection of the new Cabinet.

Taft's true interests in this matter were not what they might normally have been expected to be. Given not only his own rejection at the convention but also the way it had been brought about, any other politician would have been deeply determined that at minimum the new administration must make room for authentically Taft Republicans right at the top. But this was not Taft's demand at all. To be sure, he was briefly annoyed when, at the urging of liberal Republicans, Eisenhower chose a leader of a plumbers' union, Martin Durkin, as his first Secretary of Labor. This appointment caused Taft to gulp in disbelief and to mutter, "Incredible! Incredible!" But it was a routine protest, made more to object that the Prime Minister had not been consulted than because Taft had any strong feelings in the matter.

He was not really much concerned about such arrangements, whether as to purposes or as to personnel, that Eisenhower might contemplate in the area of domestic affairs. For Taft had no doubt that in this field he himself would be able to prevent the administration from becoming too un-Republican by his standards, and had he lived longer there is little doubt that his estimate would have been correct. The core of his resolve lay elsewhere. It was in the area of foreign policy.

He had long distrusted Eisenhower's intimate relationship with the Eastern Establishment in world affairs and notably and poignantly his empathy with the strongly Europe First concept that was the first article in that Establishment's credo. In this sense, Taft saw Eisenhower as only another in a fairly long line of Thomas E. Dewey types. Governor Dewey had brushed Taft aside for the Presidential nomination in 1944 and had brushed Taft types aside again in 1948, only to lose embarrassingly to Harry Truman.

Taft's vigorous dislike of "Dewey Republicans" was the nearest approach to malice shown in all his life, and this was because he saw them as only pseudo-Republicans ready to pander to Democrats and, most of all, uncritically to swallow Democratic foreign-policy dogmas that he thought to be objectively questionable. He saw them as politically servile; and he honestly considered, too, that this "me-too" approach was a denial of the central meaning of the two-party system and amounted, in fact, to a deprivation of the right and duty of the voters to make conscious choices between genuine alternatives on the higher public issues.

Thus, suspecting Eisenhower of being Democratic just below the skin on foreign policy, Taft's grand purpose at the start was to turn the President away from this attitude, both by personal intervention and by a judicious use of the Taft influence in the matter of Eisenhower's foreign-military policy appointments.

The choice by Eisenhower of John Foster Dulles was highly pleasing to Taft. This was not because Dulles in his brief career as an elected politician in the Senate had been a Taft man—he had not been. It was because Taft knew that the real Dulles was neither unduly preoccupied with purely European problems nor in the faintest way soft toward the grisly challenge to American interests which Taft clearly saw rising in Asia. It cannot be said, of course, that Taft *caused* the appointment of Dulles to the State Department in any direct sense. At the time, actually, the vague and general estimate was that Dulles's true home was probably next door to, if not in, the home of the Europe-Firsters. But Taft knew very much better than this, and Taft's influence was subtly employed in Dulles's behalf. So, concurrent with the appointment, Taft told his people that they could feel both safe and vindicated in their own foreign views. Accepting the then general assumption that because Taft had disagreed with Dulles on the wisdom of NATO Eisenhower's choice of Dulles was a blow to the Senator, a journalistic friend inquired of him, "Will Foster Dulles really do, from your point of view?"

"Will he do?" Taft responded with a smile. "Oh, yes, indeed yes; very, very satisfactory indeed." Then he turned his right hand in the gesture of a man closing a valve and added, "You see, I understand Foster very well; and Foster understands me."

Again, the Taft power so arcanely exercised in the Dulles appointment was applied with total and unabashed openness when the time came for the appointment of a new Chairman of the Joint Chiefs of Staff. Here, Taft went at his problem headlong and with not the slightest dissimulation. One late afternoon just off the floor of the Senate he called me over to where he was sitting and said, in a very causal way, "Like to know who's going to be the new chairman of the JCS?" The reply was, of course, affirmative. "Here," said Taft, "look at this." He handed over a crumpled envelope on which was written the single name "Radford."

"It's going to be Radford," he remarked. "I have just been out to the Wardman Park Hotel to *notify* Charlie Wilson of that." Charles Wilson, late of General Motors, was Eisenhower's Secretary of Defense. Admiral Arthur Radford, a leading exponent both of air power (Taft's central military faith) and of a hard line against Communist expansion in Asia (Taft's irreducible foreign-policy concept), within a few days was publicly revealed as the new Chairman of the Joint Chiefs.

And the Admiral was a Taft man in precisely the sense that Taft wanted his admirers to *be* Taft men: honorable, able, independent, a like believer but never a toady, a follower but never a stooge. Thus, the quality of high paradox that was Taft's lifelong companion in public affairs, almost invariably assisting him in the substance of the things he wanted to do impersonally and almost as invariably turning in hostility upon him when it came to his personal political ambitions, reached its zenith of improbability in the national security structure of the Eisenhower administration.

The great party spokesman on domestic affairs became in fact the moving spirit in the foreign-policy household apparatus of the very man, Eisenhower, who had taken the Presidency away from Robert Taft on the assumption that Taft did not understand foreign policy. For the truth of the business, no matter how little apprehended it was then and how unlikely it may seem now, was that so long as Taft lived to stand in the Senate the keys to the power both in the Department of State and in the Department of Defense lay in the hands of men whose *ultimate* views of a proper foreign policy were, again in truth, more nearly Taft's than Eisenhower's. Dulles and Radford, that is to say, were at bottom not exactly Asia-first types, but they were types all the same whose estimate of Communist intentions and Communist danger in Asia were far closer to Taft's than to Eisenhower's. This was almost instantly clear in the case of Radford at the Pentagon; it required longer for the same inner reality to emerge in the case of the more sophisticated man who was Dulles.

It is, of course, important to bear in mind that Taft's life span in relation to the Eisenhower administration was short and that when he died a good many things in consequence were changed. For one illustration, given a Taft alive and well in the Senate and thus in position to give to Dulles both a powerful Senatorial protection and a sharp nudge, it is extremely improbable that the Eisenhower administration would have taken up so inactive a policy toward the destruction of French Indochina, which by late 1954 was proceeding apace and which was later to see under President Johnson the commitment of more than half a million American troops to save anti-Communist South Vietnam from this Communist "war of liberation."

But all this, of course, was not to be; the duration of Taft's curious influence upon affairs was fated to be as short as it was profound. For it was only weeks after the Eisenhower administration came in that Taft, Taft the tireless, Taft the heedless of personal comfort or personal health, Taft the eighteen-hour-a-day worker who habitually took a great mass of dull papers home at night, sickened imperceptibly before the eyes of his colleagues. It may well be thought in retrospect that the appalling nature of his rejection for the Presidency had bitten deeper into him than anybody, even Martha Taft, would ever know, and that, unlike Harry Truman and Lyndon Johnson, his capacity to throw off ultimate despair in the face of cruel and monumental unfairness was more apparent on the outside than real on the inside.

It is, perhaps, at least a fair speculation. For Taft by the softer, far more privileged circumstances of his life and background was never so essentially resistant a man as was either Harry Truman—"the little bastard with the iron gut," as an old friend inelegantly said of him—or Lyndon Baines Johnson, who had come up from the bleak, poor hills of South Texas and had in him the incomparable toughness of a stoic pioneer stock that had fought other Englishmen and Indians and Mexicans—and Yankees—and had every time risen to fight again.

At all events, Taft's own powers of resistance left him like water seeping from a suddenly broken canteen. One day he was in seeming vigor; a day or two hence and the faint lines of hidden pain became visible in his always too pale, irregularly rounded and domed and shyly closed face. Once the cancer entered his body ("the damnedest damn thing that ever got ahold of me," his old institutional antagonist, Speaker Sam Rayburn of Texas, was to say later when he, too, was dying of the same complaint), its fatal progression was sure and rapid. Taft spoke of it never; and treated the thing, to all outward appearances, as a kind of bad cold. Still, by May 1953— a little while after he had made a laconic golfing trip with President Eisenhower to Augusta, Georgia—he was forced to enter Walter Reed hospital in Washington for what, characteristically finding the least dramatic terminology he could put his tongue to, he called "a checkup."

But, of course, it was more than that, far more than that, and he emerged from the hospital on crutches. For two months he knew that he was going to die; but he told no one save old Herbert Hoover. To Hoover he said one day, "I know what I've got and you know what I've got; I'm going to die with my boots on." But this he did not quite do, except metaphorically. On the night of July 31 he fell into a coma; at 11:30 o'clock the next morning his life came to its close.

The funeral was, as the saying goes, a splendid one; and the common expression of the time was, inevitably, that with Taft's end an era had ended as well. Still, this was not quite the right of it. Taft never quite symbolized an era, nor did he ever master one. In a way, he was always the odd man out, a man forever with people and forever alone. But if he never made an era, he gave singular honor, for all his faults and shortcomings, to a profession forever vilified but forever needed. Perhaps the way to put it is to say of him that he was of all of them the most unprofessional of the professional Responsibles.

· · ·

BOOK FOUR

Dwight D. Eisenhower

• • •

One of the more high-toned clichés of politics is that sometimes, at least, the deep needs of the nation will form a perfect, if unconscious, union with the man most suited to meet them, by a process of fate or fortuity. The devout will see in it all the workings of Providence; the skeptic as simply a fortunate roll of the great dice of blind circumstance.

Whether by divine will or sheer accident, Dwight David Eisenhower was the most profound human embodiment of the essential truth of this cliché. For this sometimes wholly ingenuous and limpidly clear man, this sometimes opaquely unreadable man in both his syntax and his inner purposes, arrived upon the American political scene much as though he had sprung from the forehead of some cosmic dramatist determined to write a play in which the hero fitted perfectly, without an overlapping edge anywhere, into the conditions of his time and place.

III

If it was on the whole a play of a certain dullness, lacking both in somberness and splendor, it was also a play with an appositeness so total as to be without example in the American theater of public affairs.

For both as politician and as President, Dwight Eisenhower was in a superficial way the admiral who hated the sea. He was a latecoming politician who, on the outside, scorned and shrank from any taint of expertise in the profession to which somehow he had been called. He actively disliked those he called, pejoratively, "practical politicians"; and in eight years in the highest office he was at some pains to avoid any suggestion of urgent concern for his trade.

As a President, he was master of a form of seemingly relaxed leadership which, again on the surface, was most of all notable for a long recoil from any close personal identification with the qualities of creativity or passion or "commitment." He was, on all the external evidence, the first chief executive we ever had to apply to all his problems and designs an attitude which a subsequent beatnik generation would beatify in the shrine of its values with the term "cool." And yet the whole of humankind could be searched in vain for any man more antithetical to and uncomprehending of "coolness" in its beatnik context.

For nearly everything that appeared to be the reality about Dwight Eisenhower was itself an immense illusion, a kind of distorting mirror wholly false to the truth of it all. For he was in fact, if one goes by the unalterable record and not by the absurd legends that so grew up about him, one of the most competent, and certainly one of the most persistently beloved, Presidents of all time. To understand him at all, either as politician or President, it is first of all necessary to accept the improbable and resolutely to ignore the plausible. His was the saga of a triumphant illogic which became a higher logic. He reached the Presidency by not seeking it—except that, in fact, he made it come to him. He performed in the Presidency by acting always as though it would be perfectly all right with him if someone else had got the job. He appealed to the voters not so much by asking them for their support as by indicating, though in a very modest and throwaway style, that he was willing to serve them if they really wanted him to; but that, anyhow, it would surely all come out all right one way or the other. His manner, faintly but never arrogantly, suggested what his mouth never did—that they would be pretty lucky to get him. And this, in plain truth, as it turned out, they were.

He broke almost every rule in the politician's handbook with offhand unconcern. He never scolded pressure groups, of whatever kind; he simply let them know, again and again, that of course he would do what was "right." And, usually, what he thought was right was precisely what they thought was very wrong. And, incredible as it sounds—and as it actually was—nobody and no interest group ever got very angry at him. If a certain irascibility was from time to time directed at him, it had two highly qualifying aspects. First of all, it did not endure; and second, he never showed the slightest anxiety about it.

In the days of his power (always carefully muted and more or less apologized for) and of his glory (always accepted as though it was just one of those things and not altogether a comfortable thing at that) a whole generation of politicians in both parties looked upon him with an almost comical sense of wonder and incredulity, as though a horse had become airborne or a tree had begun to stroll about the landscape. His sense of humor was far from acute, and certainly never highly developed. It was, in truth, mostly the humor of the bridge table or the country club; it was never the least mordant and never memorably clever or touched by any sense of irony in the classic sense. And yet, it is possible in looking back, without being fanciful, to suspect that the view so widely held of him by his politician-colleagues gave him great amusement—inside. Outwardly, he was grave and sober; he never ridiculed anybody.

The "pols" generally, and poignantly so those in his own party, could never figure him out, from first to last. They fell at length into the general view that he was simply *sui generis*—that "they broke the mold when they made Ol' Ike"—as they did. He was not merely a man in a million; he was a man in two hundred million.

He was in the political world somewhat remindful of Edgar Allan Poe's literary aphorism of the Purloined Letter. To the country he displayed nearly everything of himself and of his actions and plans, speaking with a mélange of diction that was part Old Army, part Federal bureaucratese, part paternal, part hortatory, part inspirational and part the language of the most undeniable simple good will. It all came out in an appalling mix of rhetoric, but everybody understood it perfectly on one level, the level of what he was doing and why. Practically nobody ever understood it on another level, the level that expressed Dwight Eisenhower as he really was. Eisenhower the real man was quite misapprehended; if he knew it, it never bothered him in the least. The people, that is to say, found one of the letters that he had tossed atop the bureau; they never even knew the other was there. For the message of the other, the unfound letter, told of the extraordinary skill of this professional soldier turned amateur politician; indeed, it actually told, had anyone much been able to read it, that he was far abler as a politician—and yes, statesman—than he had ever been as a soldier.

As a soldier he was a dullish type, honorable, obedient to higher authority, limited in imagination and very careful not to "get out of line," in all of his peacetime Army service. Fortune and circumstance put their hand upon his shoulder as the Second World War was reaching its climax in the preparations for the grand assault across the English Channel upon Hitler's stolen Fortress Europe. Because the Allied invading forces being assembled in Britain were necessarily heavily American in origin, because Winston Churchill of Britain was immensely concerned to keep the best of all possible relationships with President Franklin D. Roosevelt, and because Roosevelt was in trouble here at home with forces that wanted to fight the Pacific war first and give second place to the contest for Europe, a great light fell near Christmastime in 1943 upon the theretofore undistinguished career of an erstwhile lieutenant colonel called Dwight David Eisenhower.

The Roosevelt-Churchill concern was to find an officer

to hold supreme command of the Allied armies who would be adequate in the fields but no less than superb in the real job of it all. This was to maintain, to foster and to improve the working relationships between the British and Commonwealth and American troops now so restively waiting in England for D-Day and H-Hour. They had, in a word, a supreme problem of their own. In long and short, it was the transcendental problem of keeping the Alliance itself together.

Churchill had no lack of able generals. There was Sir Harold Alexander (later Earl Alexander of Tunis), and there was Bernard Montgomery (later Earl Montgomery of Alamein). But Alexander was by this time indispensable to Churchill's whole war strategy in what was from first to last the central of all his preoccupations. This was the liberation and the consolidation under Allied power of the basin of the Mediterranean. Montgomery, the hero of great desert battles in North Africa, was the irreplaceable symbol of the storied British Eighth Army, but he was also a difficult fellow and one notably unloved by Winston Churchill. Montgomery was "Monty" or "Super-Monty" to the popular press, but to the aristocratic, cavalier-born, whisky-and-brandy-drinking Prime Minister this spare, vain tiresomely talkative, excessively puritanical and ridiculously abstemious Scot was a poor bit of goods.

Moreover, Churchill was not in any case in any position whatever to insist upon a British Commander in Chief for D-Day and all the rest of it; nor would Roosevelt, for that matter, for a moment have agreed to such an arrangement. The sheerly objective circumstances would plainly have dictated the choice of General George C. Marshall, then the U.S. Army chief of staff, a man who had held general-officer rank when Eisenhower was, as they said in the Army, just a pup. But Roosevelt was having a very hard time at home in rightly insisting upon a grand war policy of Europe First. The old isolationist forces had still no love for the concept of "Europe." More important, the savage Japanese attack upon our main fleet at Pearl Harbor had sent through the whole rank and file of the nation a passionate will for revenge and a profound belief that the first enemy was Emperor Hirohito rather than Adolf Hitler. In order, then, to be able to sustain the central strategy of Europe First—and also to keep close at hand for unending counsel the man who was to be indispensable to the ultimate American victory—Roosevelt felt that he could not send Marshall off to Europe.

It thus fell out that Dwight Eisenhower became Commander in Chief of the greatest, the most massive and the most critical military action in warfare. That the choice was fortuitous is true enough; but it was to turn out that it was also extremely wise. For Eisenhower, who had spent so many years in uniform without ever having heard a gun fired outside the rifle range, astonished his professional detractors and infinitely comforted his great patrons—"Franklin and Winnie"—by the quality of his leadership.

He managed to move in over the heads of dozens of far senior officers without leaving among them a single enduring breach—where even a single breach would have been damaging to Allied designs. In the seemingly eternal months in England while the old Allied secret planning headquarters called Cossack was being slowly transformed into something that would become Overlord (the code name for the gathering push of D-Day), he accomplished an absolute, a literal, marvel in forever destroying the old, cynical adage that the best way to lose a war was to have Allies. This compact, ruddy, nearly always smiling man with a highly un-English name and cultural heritage (it was basically Swiss or Swiss-German) became quite simply beloved of British civilians and politicians and acceptable even to such stern Land of Hope and Glory fellows as the officers of the Royal Navy—not to mention the then lions of the hour in the Royal Air Force.

Everywhere he went he carried an aura of firmness mixed with geniality, of pride mixed with humility. Like other war correspondents standing around in England and waiting for D-Day, I saw the General occasionally, though no claim is here entered that he ever saw me. Every officers' mess was full of scuttlebut about his miracle in welding the essentially disparate American and British combat types into a single force. And most of the scuttlebut was true.

There was, for illustration, an occasion in which he abruptly sent an American general home on the slowest boat that could be found. Why? Well, it seemed that the American had called his English opposite number a "British son of a bitch." The story went—and it was not apocryphal—that Eisenhower had told his fellow American officer: "I'm not sending you home because you called So-and-So a son of a bitch; it's because you called him a *British* son of a bitch."

Though Eisenhower as Commander in Chief manfully took many hard decisions of high command, these were neither his chief contributions nor always products of hard choice so much as of harder necessity. When foul weather broke the Allies' original plan to sally forth from England on June 5, 1944, for example, it is quite true that Eisenhower had to bear alone the responsibility for deciding that H-Hour should come the next day, weather or not. It is, however, fair to say that he had no real option here; the whole coast of England was all but sinking under our massed machines of war, and once this' juggernaut had been cranked up it could hardly have been long arrested in any case.

The core of the whole business was that he was never, in fact, really a soldier as most think of the great captain —a hard-bitten, gung-ho combat type with mud on his boots and implacable attack in his heart. He was no George Patton, no Courtney Hodges, and for that matter no Montgomery, and likely never could have been. But he was a great deal more. He was a kind of lofty field marshal for the incomparably higher and more subtle responsibility of keeping an alliance intact and of serving as unguent between the egos of Churchill and Roosevelt.

Never in history had two heads of state owed so much to one man. For if classical soldiers like Alexander and Douglas MacArthur had forgotten more about the science of warfare than Eisenhower was ever likely to learn, he had an expertise in dealing with the root realities of it all of which neither ever dreamed. He was, in short, the first master in our time of the incredibly complex art of the soldier-politician, or, indeed, of the soldier-statesman. He was a kind of prairie Caesar of modern times; a modest Caesar, to be sure, but all the same a very longlooking one.

Once this writer attempted, in an article in *Harper's* while Eisenhower was President, to suggest this distinction. Whether the President ever even saw the article could be mooted, in view of his consistent policy of avowed public inattentiveness to this sort of thing, though I have my own notions as to the right answer. In any event, by mere happenstance or not, an iron curtain shortly descended in the White House so far as a journalist named William S. White was concerned. And it never lifted until, years later, the same journalist had defended President Eisenhower on a series of foreign-policy issues. How to explain it that a President would prefer to be called a good soldier to something far, far higher than a good soldier? How indeed? Perhaps one could refer back to Harry S. Truman, who was deeply offended at being termed a poor politician but also a very great President?

The Eisenhower who could speak in the crisis conferences inside the White House with a brusque and total lucidity—with which he could also write, when he chose —could speak in press conferences with an all but insoluble patois of his own. On one very hot day he was meeting the press in the ornately rococo Treaty Room of the old State-War-Navy building in Washington, and some of the correspondents had put aside their jackets. Several hands were raised by prospective questioners but the President's eye fell upon Russell Baker of the *New York Times*. Rising to put his inquiry, Baker found himself in contention with several others similarly disposed. He paused, politely, but Eisenhower shook his head negatively at the others and said, "No, no—that man there that has the shirt on."

Indeed, some of us would not engage to write about what he had said until we had seen a full transcript of the press conference—a transcript characteristically and uncaringly honest, with all the Eisenhower rhetorical warts preserved intact. From this and other evidence, including calculated leaks from the White House to the effect that the President read very little of anything and practically nothing of what the press might choose or not choose to write, there arose the story that he was a Philistine and proud of it. The truth, which I later learned on what is usually called the most unimpeachable authority, is that Eisenhower was nothing of the kind. With a practical wisdom that was sadly lacking in the cases of both Presidents John Kennedy and Lyndon Johnson, Eisenhower had made up his mind early in the game that the way to reduce the slings and arrows from the press was simply to take up the position that he had never heard of this or that article or column in the first place. Thus deflating his critics with a sophisticated one-upmanship that was, again superficially, alien to him, he licked his press wounds entirely in private—with some exceptions.

It is true that when he reached the settled conclusion that Columnist A or Correspondent B was what he felt to be persistently "unreliable" or "irresponsible"—the only two really unforgivable sins in his credo—he would never again read another word from that man, nor gladly tolerate any discussion of any kind that might involve him. An associate once brought to his attention the column of a man thus condemned, and Eisenhower instantly showed the high temper which very few Americans ever knew he had. "Damn it," he said furiously, "if all you have got to do is to read that goddamn ass how in the hell can you get your work done?"

Similarly, legend and reality were two quite different things in connection with his relationship to his Vice-President, Richard Nixon. It was persistently put about that Eisenhower had never really liked Nixon; and for that matter it was quite true that in the 1952 campaign he had been considerably less than kind and compassionate toward his Vice-Presidential designee when Nixon got into trouble over a so-called "special fund" raised for him by California business interests to help defray his heavy expenses as a Senator. It was quite true, that is, that Eisenhower was not too sympathetic until Nixon, in his famous "Checkers" radio and television speech to the country, had not only evoked an unexampled response of public trust and pity but had emerged, in Eisenhower's view, as "clean as a hound's tooth," and also as an obvious carrier of strength to the ticket.

Parenthetically, Eisenhower never saw in this episode anything other than an exercise of his obvious responsibility to see that Nixon was, indeed, "clean" and never understood that anything in his early attitude justified any resentment whatever on Nixon's part. (That it did cause such a resentment, and pretty understandably, too, is this writer's firm conviction; but anyhow that is another tale altogether.)

At all events, the position long *was* that Eisenhower was widely (if absolutely incorrectly) seen as far from enchanted with Richard Nixon, and great play of this supposed circumstance was made, to Nixon's harm, in the 1960 Presidential election, in which he was the Republican nominee. Asked at a press conference to enumerate such of Nixon's actions as had amounted to distinguished public service, Eisenhower's tongue perceptibly faltered and at length he got off a garrulous reply which was plainly translatable to mean, "Give me a week and I can think of something."

The question had been put at the very end of the conference, with an air of confusion in the room that was invariable in the circumstances, and Eisenhower had no time, first, to correct himself or, second, really to evaluate the nature of his reply. The fact, though unluckily for Nixon it was never put on the public record, was that the President was suffering from the third of his serious illnesses, and while his thought processes were unimpaired he was sometimes having difficulty, common in heart and stroke patients, in articulating clearly what he meant to say.

The further fact, of course, was that the President surely did not wish to suggest that he was actually incapable of saying what he meant—which would have been not only embarrassing but quite untrue. More important, he was thinking, as always he did in the really big things, of the welfare of the country and of its position abroad. Not to correct this matter in public was undeniably damaging to Richard Nixon; to correct it in public, however, would have been undeniably damaging to something much higher—the vital interests of the United States of America in a Western world looking desperately to it for leadership. So Eisenhower made his choice, and the right one it was.

The incident was brilliantly if unintentionally illustrative of one of the great strengths of his Presidency. This, to put it somewhat brutally, was that he never, never allowed any personal consideration, including the consideration of personal "loyalty" as it is commonly defined, to get for an instant into the way of what he thought he had to do as the leader of this nation. He was neither a cruel man nor a false friend; but his whole life, even before he assumed the Presidency, had taught him the hard lesson that the individual welfare of any and every man had to give way, at whatever cost, to the ultimate safety and interests of the country, of the many.

His almost invariable response when any member of his administration got into trouble or scandal, whether the scandal involved real or only alleged monetary impropriety, was to cut off that man's head. Nor did the supposed offender really have to be guilty in Eisenhower's eyes; he only had to *seem* guilty. One of the sharpest examples of this (and the sharpest in more senses than one) occurred in the case of perhaps the most powerful White House assistant of all time, former Governor Sherman Adams of New Hampshire. Adams had given rarely matched service to the President from the 1952 nominating convention onward and in the White House had become an irreplaceable gray eminence, generally, if also incorrectly, assumed in Washington pretty much to run the domestic affairs of this country.

But Adams fell into a measure of disrepute in an alleged conflict-of-interest scandal with a sharp New England business type called Bernard Goldfine, and before very long the hound's tooth, as Eisenhower had called it, was no longer so clean. Adams was brusquely dismissed, through the customary euphemistic device of "resignation." And on the very same day Eisenhower, as he records in his memoirs, *The White House Years*, gave to the departing servant a silver bowl thus inscribed:

FOR TIRELESS SERVICE TO THE PUBLIC
BRILLIANT PERFORMANCE OF EVERY DUTY
AND
UNSURPASSED DEDICATION TO HIS COUNTRY
FROM HIS DEVOTED FRIEND
DWIGHT D. EISENHOWER.

If there was an arresting irony in this fulsome salute to a man just kicked out of the White House, it was also pure, authentic Eisenhower. Harry Truman would never have done quite such a thing, public pressure or no public pressure (though Franklin Roosevelt would have and did, in the same spirit if not quite in the same literal circumstances). John Kennedy would never have done it. Lyndon Johnson would never have done it. All the same, all three of them would have been wrong; for no private interest, not even the private emotion of great affection and loyalty given and repaid, can be allowed to stand in the way of the public interest.

This Eisenhower always understood and always acted upon. Indeed, the fact is that while no sane man could have ever called him unfeeling, he did have about him, as do many men of uncommon prudence and rectitude and uncommon public renown for it, a harshly demanding attitude toward the targets or mere victims of the Mrs. Grundys of politics. He believed in cutting his losses, but only because his losses were the country's losses. It is a hard concept, but also a necessary one. In Eisenhower's case it was followed with complete impersonality and without the smallest lessening of his private esteem for the man caught up in its operation. When he said all those glowing things about Sherman Adams, he meant them, every word.

But in warfare he had sent countless thousands to bitter sacrifice and death and he had done what he had to do without sentimentality, nor ever a false tear for having discharged the duty laid upon him in the way he thought he must. Indeed, it was the war and Eisenhower's matchless part in it that became the training ground for his Presidency, much as the Senate of the United States had been for Harry Truman, for John Kennedy, for Lyndon Johnson and, in part at least, for Richard Nixon, too. For Eisenhower went without a hitch or bobble from supreme command of the Allied invasion forces in Europe to supreme command of Columbia University and to supreme command of the North Atlantic Treaty Organization—and, finally, to supreme command of the United States of America. Always, or until nearly the very end, he protested an absence of political ambition. Always, he was seen as being dragged reluctantly into political history. Always he gained it all by seeming to want nothing at all, until at last he had it all—and had it all twice.

Two interpretations are clearly possible. One is that he was simply a very tricky man who was biding his time and had read enough of political lore to learn that an overt thirst for the Presidency was frowned upon as not playing the game—as it used not to be. The other is—and it is adopted by this writer upon the most mature consideration—that his earlier protestations were more genuine than not but that high place came to him rather in the sense that it came to those generals in Napoleon's Grande Armée who had that special, that indefinable thing called good luck.

The hypothetical strength of Theory No. 1 is of course not inconsiderable. The strength of Theory No. 2 is entirely palpable, is wholly visible. For Eisenhower's conduct, at Columbia University and at NATO, *was* professionally correct altogether, as for that matter it had been correct in all his Army career. There is no room for genuine doubt that he really *didn't* want the Presidency, in any sense that could be called merely clever or in any motivation that could be called quietly conniving. He really did at length enter the lists mainly because he was concerned at what he honestly believed to be an unwise drift of public affairs in this country.

For somewhere along the line of what had been on the whole a remarkably untroubled life and an utterly undoctrinaire view of that life, he undoubtedly had evolved a political philosophy of moderation, of centrism, as he had, of course, always held a sense of untroubled patriotism and of the duty of serving when called upon. This is not meant to suggest that he was only some middle-aged Boy Scout, forever reciting the Pledge of Allegiance to the Flag and forever doing good works in a bad, bad world. If he was in some respects a simple man, he was never a simplistic man.

It used to be said of him, particularly in his first term as President, that he was only a military fellow who had read the Constitution too late in life and naïvely really believed such of its admonitions as its demand for a government of divided powers and of checks and balances. It used to be said of him, too, as it was once half-jokingly said by a journalistic colleague of mine, that the President's real literary preferences were for the works of such authors as Zane Grey. These estimates, and not Eisenhower's alleged copybook attitudes toward the Constitution and life, were, of course, the real inanities here. For he was, after all, right about what the Constitution says; and as to his level of "culture" he was very far from a dolt and perfectly at home with the brightest of minds and talents—when he chose to be.

But, like all men, he was, when all was said and done, the product of all he had been, and this explained what some considered to be the active "anti-intellectualism" of his regime. They forgot, in saying this, that in his actions as distinguished from his "aura"—sometimes an aura in no way of his own making—he consistently defended free thought everywhere in his nation, not excluding in his own official family. They forgot also that while he tirelessly proclaimed the right and proper "independence" of Congress, he never had any hesitation in putting his own bland version of the squeeze upon Congress *when he really wanted something*. This is to say, when he really wanted something from Congress dealing with

foreign affairs. For his reading of the Constitution, however late in life this may have occurred, left him with
more than one message; it left him also with the message
that he, the President, had the right and the duty to ⌐
conduct the foreign affairs of the United States. And this
he did.

His march to the Presidency in 1952, which he somehow made more a gracious acceptance on his part than
any nasty struggle for personal power and place, was, as
has been related, made over the broken political bodies
of Senator Robert A. Taft and of the whole school of
traditional, Midwestern "regular" Republicanism. But
like the good Responsible he was and like the good high
commander he had long before been in England, Eisenhower shrank instinctively from any rubbish about unconditional victory on his side or unconditional surrender on the other side. By the time the Republican
National Convention had ended in the summer he had
already made up his mind, in the strangely allusive and
oblique way in which sometimes it worked, that he
would be a President of reunion, of rehealing; a chief
executive presiding over lowered political temperatures,
inside his own party as well as out. The truth is that
while he was at some pains to proclaim, from time to
time, the purity of his Republicanism and the long-
standing nature of his embrace of same, he recognized
the central fact that winning the Presidency was one
thing and operating the Presidency was quite another
thing.

So prior to the onset of the active campaigning of the
fall, he had gone about, much as he had done in wartime

Britain, salving wounds of pride everywhere, summoning the disaffected Republican Old Guard to the central duty of gaining office, and agreeing with them, but only to a nicely calculated point, that *certain* Democrats were perhaps SOBs. But, he suggested in substance, there were really not many of these; and in any case what was this country all about if people couldn't disagree heartily without hating at all?

Here he was, a resolute amateur surrounded by serried hordes of Republican pros and entering a kind of warfare that he had never known. No campaigner ever listened to more advisers in more places on more subjects, though not always gladly so. For the Dwight Eisenhower of that broad, luminous, deeply kind and avuncular grin was also a Dwight Eisenhower with a military vocabulary of curse words that could take the skin off a political pro no less than an Army mule. Everybody told him endlessly what to do and say, and most of the time he wound up doing and saying exactly what he pleased. He had been, from Normandy on, a great favorite with the opposition Democrats themselves (including Harry S. Truman, who would have been far from distressed had Eisenhower become the *Democratic* nominee), and he never had the slightest intention to open any blood feud with the Democratic party, any more than earlier he had had with Robert Taft.

This was the era of the McCarthy rampage, of the wild sorties against due process of Senator Joseph McCarthy; and the liberal wing of the Republican party, plus formidable allies among Eisenhower Democrats, were desperately concerned that "the General" should treat that ugly phenomenon with the plainest of denunciation and contempt. So it was that when Eisenhower went campaigning in Wisconsin all these forces assumed that he would surely take on McCarthy. This he declined to do, and at almost the last minute, though he did on one occasion defend his old mentor, General George Marshall, from collateral assaults put in by collateral McCarthyites.

The "betrayal" in Wisconsin offended—but not enduringly—the anti-McCarthy people; and any like thing by any other Presidential candidate would have surely repelled millions of voters. Nothing of the kind happened in Eisenhower's case. This was simply because it became widely apparent that his refusal to speak out was in no sense to condone McCarthyism but proceeded instead entirely from the General's belief that sometimes the best way to get rid of a nuisance was to refuse resolutely to grant it any attention whatever. In short, Eisenhower was forgiven, as many another would never have been, because of the wide public instinct of what Eisenhower really was. It was not so with the more sophisticated observers; it took a good while for this writer himself, for one, not to see this episode as an unpleasant one, to say the least. It took, in other words, the space of time that intervened until the Eisenhower in office began to come through as a man of genuine devotion to and concern for civil liberties and to fairness in both public discourse and political contention.

This, again, is only another way of returning to the central point: that Eisenhower was a unique public man. Not long after his own election, President John Kennedy paid a visit to Eisenhower's lush estate at Gettysburg and came away wide-eyed at the valuable gifts of many kinds which the former President had accepted with the utmost of unselfconsciousness from rich friends. "My God," said Kennedy to me, "if Lyndon or I had accepted this kind of thing we'd probably be impeached."

Because Eisenhower could not conceive either that he *could* be improperly influenced by any gift or that anybody else could conceivably suppose that he could be, he took it for granted that presents to him from friends were simply that—from friend to friend. Quite probably, he was entirely right in this. For to those who knew him the spectacle of influence-peddling within sight or sound of Dwight David Eisenhower, even apart from the fact that his donors were generally among the most distinguished and honorable men in the United States, carried a total implausibility.

To be sure, it is undoubtedly true that he had a curiously strong affinity for rich men, as guests and companions but by no means always as practical advisers. So much was this the case that the White House social lists for his dinner parties almost always carried a disproportionate number of the names of those who had been merely commercially successful. His enchantment with men of wealth was not, however, so much materialistically based as a reflection of his fixed belief that nobody got up there in the upper brackets without having a great deal of good sense.

An old Eisenhower backer, former Senator James Duff of Pennsylvania, once explained the phenomenon to me in this way: "When Eisenhower wrote his first book [*Crusade in Europe*] he was in fact an amateur writer and so the income-tax people allowed him the capital-gains formula rather than applying the income-tax bite. The result, of course, was that he made a good deal of money—about a quarter of a million, as I recall.

"Now, about that time some of his friends in banking and all that sort of thing went to see him, while he was at Columbia, and told him they would like to invest his money for him. It was, of course, absolutely on the up and up, but it is also true that these fellows knew their way around the stock market. The upshot was that Ike's quarter of a million became a great deal bigger; and he was just like a kid who had first learned that money can make money if you know how.

"Hell," Duff added, with a wry grin, "any damn fool can make a million dollars, but the President just doesn't know that. An Army man nearly all his life—he just doesn't know the money game."

Perhaps the President really didn't know his way around in corporate finance and was overly impressed with those who did. (Perhaps, too, Duff's anecdote was overdrawn a bit in the human desire to make a point interestingly.) One thing at least, however, Eisenhower certainly did know. This was how to keep his communications open with the more mercantile and more right-wing Republican types without ever sacrificing to this political need anything of substance or principle. Against a persistently niggling doubt among these people that "Ike's" Republicanism was really quite soundly orthodox, he did just enough and said just enough to lull their suspicions, but never any more. He would, for illustration, enchant them occasionally with observations to the effect that perfect personal "security" could be found only in prison, or that he himself had been of a poor family that "never knew it was poor." Constantly, too, he talked up the pristine virtues of balanced budgets and "reduced Federal spending," intoning with faithful ritualism the litanies of old-fashioned conservatism in such matters. When it came to action, however, it was a different matter. Resolutely, and effectively, he consistently fought off the budget-balancers on such grand topics as foreign aid and, for that matter, even domestic welfarism.

Not from its beginning to its end did his administration attempt any repeal of the massive social legislation that had been put upon the books in the Roosevelt and Truman years. Not from its beginning to its end was his administration ever penny-pinching in attitude or performance, though here, too, Eisenhower would now and again throw a semantical bone to the right wing of the GOP. He had a Republican-controlled Congress at his back for only two of his eight years, and these two were in fact his most difficult years. His own triumph of 1952 had hardly been won before the Republicans lost Congress in the elections of 1954, never again to regain it in his time.

He was far better off in the latter six years because of two realities. The first was that he had never intended in any event to attempt to reverse the generally liberal trend of all the Congresses since Roosevelt. The second was, simply, that his true and all but exclusive interest actually lay from the beginning in the field of world affairs. In this matter of total urgency the Congressional Democrats, and notably such powers as Majority Leader Lyndon Johnson in the Senate and Speaker Sam Rayburn of the House of Representatives, spoke Eisenhower's language and shared Eisenhower's crucial concerns far more than did the common run of his own party. So what really happened was this: From 1954 onward, Eisenhower was spared the pain and peril of having to deal gingerly with such sturdily traditional Republican leaders as Senators William F. Knowland of California and Styles Bridges of New Hampshire.

Knowland and Bridges held the liveliest of skepticism about a good many of Eisenhower's foreign-policy designs, notably in such issues as his persistent efforts to make practical accommodations with such of the Iron Curtain countries in Eastern Europe as were showing some signs of ideological recoil from the harsh Stalinism of Moscow. Both being men who deeply feared what they believed to be Eisenhower's unwisely sunny view of the nature of the Communist menace, they never hesitated to challenge the President's leadership.

But once the Democrats lodged themselves into Congressional control, Eisenhower had only to go to Johnson and Rayburn to secure a rare cooperation on international affairs. This helpfulness Johnson in the Senate extended with entire naturalness, because he was not in any case an instinctive partisan and, of course, because he considered Eisenhower to be in the right. In consequence, there grew up between the two native Texans (Eisenhower's birthplace was in North Texas) a warm and personal collaboration, limited to foreign affairs by mutual consent, which literally saved Eisenhower as President many times—and which was later of immense assistance to Lyndon Johnson when *he* became President. Indeed, the Eisenhower out of office was hardly less important in some ways—for example, in his steadfast and unpartisan defense of Johnson in the Vietnam War—than the Eisenhower in office had been.

Rayburn's helpfulness to the Eisenhower Presidency was of a different form altogether. More partisan by nature than Johnson, Rayburn helped the man he called "Captain Ike" on every foreign crisis but plainly never enjoyed doing it and from time to time would roundly curse the circumstances of fate that compelled him to do in the higher national interest what he would very much like not to have done. "Goddamn it," he would say of an evening to a friend in the "Rayburn Board of Education" —which is to say at cocktail time in his most private of House offices—"my back is gettin' mighty sore."

Eisenhower, of course, knew of the difference in spirit between Johnson's and Rayburn's assistance to him and he never got nearly so humanly close to "Mr. Sam." He got so close to Lyndon Johnson, to the contrary, that one would not like to bet any large sum that Dwight Eisenhower, in the privacy of the polling booth, marked his ballot in November of 1964 for the Republican candidate called Barry Goldwater rather than for a Democrat named Johnson.

In any event, the net of it was that for six years Eisenhower and the controlling Congressional Democrats operated what was in effect a coalition government, and the farther it recedes into history the better it looks. A great many men, a very great many men, who were very far from Eisenhowerites at the time have in the years since done a great deal of private brooding in a process of Revisiting Eisenhower and have come to the conclusion that no matter how he did it all, he did it very well after all.

It is perhaps not against the law to quote oneself in this connection. On the occasion of one of Eisenhower's many illnesses, and in the afterlight of his Presidency, when it looked that the old gentleman might be departing this life, I wrote a syndicatèd column to the following effect:

Dwight David Eisenhower is in his own time receiving both a vast surge of public affection and a new respect from old critics that has come to no other American leader this side of the gates of death. As a President, he was the despair of political theorists, and as the Supreme Allied Commander in Europe he was the despair of professional soldiers, to this columnist's well-remembered knowledge. For he seemed to solve great problems, in the White House or in Normandy, simply by refusing to accept their existence. And he led the Republican Party simply by seeming to be uninterested in leading it at all. He was a politician who was bored by politics and made no bones about it. He could openly yawn at partisan gatherings of high emotionalism. . . . Similarly, when national issues reached a pitch of heat he cooled them off by declining to talk about them at all, whether they involved school integration or those divisive personalities—like the late Senator McCarthy—which, as he said so many times, he did not believe in "discussing."

He came to office after a long era of "strong" Presidents in Franklin Roosevelt and Harry Truman, and sometimes he appeared bent on running the "weakest" Presidency of this century. And yet somehow there was a great design in what he did. And this, quite simply, was an irreplaceable design to lance the boils and reduce the fevers in this Nation. . . .

Writing by coincidence at about the same time, the liberal commentator Max Lerner observed that the people had trusted Eisenhower "not only because he had helped win the war but because they saw in him . . . a general with a passion for peace, a man with the common touch who had moved from the military elite into the political but seemed above the battle of the politicians."

The more-or-less conservative Richard Wilson, one of the best Washington correspondents, has summed up by saying, rightly, that Eisenhower's "clearest vision was in the great struggle for world power that engaged his whole life." This is the true heart of the matter—this President spent his whole real strength in the care and forwarding of the vital interests of this nation. It is hardly to be doubted that he was genuinely concerned with its domestic health, though I myself never thought he devoted more time to this aspect than was absolutely necessary. But what is beyond any possible doubt is that he saw his domestic programs as more important for the contributions they could make toward a stable national floor for his foreign-policy designs than for themselves.

In his farewell address upon departing the White House in 1961 he gave his own testament in these words:

"We face a hostile ideology—global in scope, atheistic in character, ruthless in purpose and insidious in method. Unhappily, the danger it poses promises to be of indefinite duration. To meet it successfully there is called for, not so much the emotional and transitory sacrifices of crisis but rather those qualities which enable us to carry forward steadily, surely and without complaint the burdens of a prolonged and complex struggle—with liberty at stake."

Now it is perfectly true that the thrust of this valedictory is debatable in contemporary times, as it is also true that this is in the rhetorical sense far from the most striking Presidential farewell in our history. Let any man judge it, in this context, precisely as he wishes. The crucial point here simply is that in common with all the Responsibles he had an absolutely clear vision of the true burden of the modern Presidency.

Thus it was that, seven years after leaving the White House, he returned again to his theme in addressing the Republican National Convention assembled in Miami Beach in the hot August of 1968. He had characteristically sat out all the preconvention maneuverings over candidates but, again characteristically, had all the same managed in some way or another to suggest that while he would, of course, be absolutely impartial there *were*, of course, certain criteria for any proper Republican Presidential nominee. These requirements, in a word, pretty well began and ended in one: the nominee must not run out on the bipartisan policy of military resistance to the Communist assault upon South Vietnam. Now nobody ever caught Eisenhower directly saying anything of this kind, but somehow everybody who counted knew that this was what was in his mind. The net of it was that he "leaned," as he himself probably would have put it had it ever been possible or needful to force him to utter on the record, to "somebody" whose initials were R.M.N.—R for Richard, M for Milhous, and N for Nixon.

The General had clearly been shaken up by the spring-time candidacies of men like Governor George Romney of Michigan, who was essentially a dove rather than a hawk on Vietnam. Those who had mastered the pursuit of Eisenhower-watching had no difficulty in grasping, too, that he had not been amused by the late switch of Governor Nelson Rockefeller of New York from the status of a moderate hawk to that of a halfway dove.

As it happened, Nixon by August had the Presidential nomination rather well in hand, in any case. Still, to make doubly sure, Eisenhower arranged to address the Republican Convention by closed television from a sick room in Walter Reed Hospital in Washington, which had become more or less his permanent home. He sternly lectured the delegates on the unwisdom of falter-ing in Vietnam, observed of the then current Soviet as-sault upon a liberalized satellite, Czechoslovakia, that it was nothing new, and then reached his peroration:

"But what is new is a growing disposition among some of us to ignore these aggressive moves, to discount the blatant threats, to seek, in effect, for surface accommoda-tions, rather than to insist upon mutual acceptance of principle. This is wishful thinking at its worst."

During this time he had been in intimate communication with President Lyndon Johnson, and what he was saying to the convention was as much directed to the anti–Vietnam War Democrats shortly to assemble in Chicago as to the Republicans in Miami Beach. He was speaking, in short, as he always really liked to speak, in support of the whole, long, bipartisan postwar philosophy for the containment of aggressive Communism, even to the point of military commitment on our side.

That he spoke also with an immense moral effectiveness is unchallengeable, whether or not one agreed with his view of the proper policy. For there never was a time in his career when a rational man could have called him the least warlike in motive, or saber-rattling in attitude. His insistence that he would be a "peace" President if elected and his insistence after election that he was in fact a "peace" President had the great strength of being the truth.

Indeed, in his early youth his family's religion had been that of an obscure sect called the River Brethren, and so far as can be made out this was basically a pacifist group which had some undoubted effect upon the young Ike, though it never convinced him. His approach to war-or-peace issues actually was so simple as to be confusing. He believed in avoiding any and every confrontation of any and every kind, whether at home or abroad, to the last possible minute and by every possible legitimate maneuver. He believed also that once confrontation was literally inevitable, once one got into whatever action was inevitable, it was manifestly foolish not to go in with whatever was required to do the job.

Thus, when in campaigning for the Presidency in 1952

he made a promise to "go to Korea," the pardonable assumption among many was that he was luxuriating in what Harry Truman sourly, and understandably, called "demagoguing." But it was not that simple. The truth, though it emerged only long afterward and never was disclosed by Eisenhower himself except in the most understated and circumspect way, was that this was much more than politics. What Eisenhower really did out there was privately to spread the word where it would do the most good—notably in Communist China—that if he reached the Presidency and the Communists went on stalling the Korean peace negotiations he would be prepared at last resort to use the atomic bomb.

He was then at length able to bring about a peace in Korea that was typically Eisenhower: It was only tolerable, as it was immediately seen, and very far from any unconditional American victory. But it did protect the integrity of the Republic of Korea and it did create an area of stability that endures to this day.

No other President in memory could have got away with just such a solution, for on all form it should have been satisfactory neither to the hard-liners nor the soft-liners. But Eisenhower did get away with it, and, as with so many other things, it looked better and better as time went on. Eisenhower's answer to criticism in this or any other field was simplicity itself; he intoned that he would never be intimidated by either "the reactionary right" or "the radical left."

It was always a question as to which side he disliked more. He thought the former to be more dangerous, particularly in its disposition to demand extreme and bomb-happy military solutions to all international dilemmas. And in this sense perhaps he detested the Right more than the Left. On the other hand, the pretensions of the Left gnawed at him, and most especially the endless denunciations by left-wing politicians of a supposedly evil thing called "power." For he knew that power was precisely what they themselves wanted most, even though sometimes unconsciously.

All his political life was spent in a kind of relaxed (but not relaxed in his lights) quarrel, naturally never expressed by him in high decibels, with what he thought of as simplistic extremisms. (He was thus a natural consensus politician, whether he was entirely conscious of this or not.) In his first State of the Union message, delivered in February 1953, when the happy Republican hordes were gathering in Washington for the first restoration since the days of the unhappy Herbert Hoover, he quietly laid down his line.

"There is, in world affairs," he said, "a steady course to be followed between an assertion of strength that is truculent and a confession of helplessness that is cowardly.

"There is, in our affairs at home, a middle way between untrammeled freedom for the individual and the demands for the welfare of the whole nation. This way must avoid government bureaucracy as carefully as it avoids neglect of the helpless."

In this there was much of paradox. It seemed to be a proclamation designed to please everybody and most unlikely to please anybody much. It did not, of course, work out that way. It pleased a great many. And collaterally there was irony here, too. For the Eisenhower who on this and on so many other occasions spoke so roundly for the glories of individualism was in fact one of the least truly individualist politicians of our time. The real Dwight Eisenhower was instead the very embodiment of a middle-class, middle-income, middle-brow, wholly unanguished revolution which with the utmost of decorum had won a place of social and political dominance in this country after the end of the Second World War.

It was essentially a corporate kind of America which they had created, if not indeed a kind of blandly decent corporation-America; and no one could possibly have better served as its symbol and head than did Eisenhower. This America had been born of the social mobility that had accompanied a wartime in which young men who in a generation before would forever have remained private soldiers had by the thousands become officers; in which relatively deprived men at home had become men of affairs and wealth; in which the old abrasions between upper and lower classes had been all but obliterated by a burgeoning middle class which had become more and more in truth a new upper-middle middle class. In short, there was no longer much of a lower class; everybody was climbing upward. Everybody, in a sense, had marched upward with Eisenhower himself.

It was not, of course, a "new elite"; such terms would have been honestly alien to the new managers who became powerful first in industry and then in politics itself. Snobbery, whether defined in the British connotation as the act of tiresomely worshipping and emulating those above, or in the American connotation as the act

144

of scornfully looking down on all those below, was no part of the spirit or thought of this newly dominant force.

What *was*, however, a deep and unalterable part of it was a vast rejection, however unconscious, of nearly every one of the real values of genuine individualism. For this, the American world of Dwight Eisenhower was most of all a world keyed to words like "cooperation," and it wholly distrusted the truly individualistic, whether in business, in the arts or in political leadership. Indeed, put against Eisenhower, Harry Truman had been an all but wild individualist—as John Kennedy and Lyndon Johnson would in their separate ways later be—and Franklin Roosevelt was in the human sense a distant lifetime away.

Moreover, Eisenhower himself in his whole career had been the antithesis of the true individualist—a "team man" in surroundings that demanded the "team" approach. Given the state of this country—a country weary of war and high endeavor and of shouting and contention—Eisenhower's emergence at its head was both historically inevitable and absolutely indispensable.

He brought to it the new gentility of the new genteels; competence; a certain unction but not too much; a sense of recoil from "confrontations" of any kind which nevertheless had in it no stain of mere timidity or uncaringness; a living, human proof of the new opportunities now open to many who not long beforehand had been members of essentially submerged, if not necessarily unhappy, castes of men. Thus it was that in his first Presidential race in 1952, and from then on as well, he was vaguely but very widely seen not as the perfect knight (for concepts of this kind were long out of American minds) but rather as the perfect gentleman.

He was, indeed, a gentleman. But he was anything but a gentleman in the old and now abandoned definition of "family" and all that. He had come from a background poor not only in money but also in what was once called social tradition, and it was not the least endearing of his traits that his background seemed never to matter to him either way. It was ironically amusing, indeed, to observe the widely current assumption, in 1952, that the country was at long last about to get rid of a rather seedy fellow in Harry Truman in favor of a real gent, who was Dwight Eisenhower. For Truman's family background was far the older and, measured by the no longer relevant criteria of the past, far more "upper," if not in some respects actually aristocratic—again by no longer applicable criteria.

It goes without saying that Eisenhower never thought of any of these nuances, and would no doubt have been appalled to see them brought forward in partial explanation of his own success. Perhaps one of the most useful of his qualities, politically, was the circumstance that he was the most nearly "American" President of his century in that his constituency was so broad both ethnically and geographically. What he inherited was a thirst for a form of national togetherness. What he brilliantly used, in the good meaning of the word, was this togetherness, with himself as both catalyst and participant in the exercise.

For one illustration, he became a convert, once he

entered politics, to the most precisely middle form of religion in this country, that of Presbyterianism. This is not to suggest that he cynically sought the shelter of the manse; it is instead to show that his whole instinct reached out for that which was not in any way extreme or even open to any suggestion that it was. Presbyterianism is "safe"—and this is said in respect and affection by one whose forebears include a long line of Presbyterian dominies. For the Presbyterian Church in general is neither toney nor *déclassé;* it is neither embarrassingly evangelistic nor yet delicately High Church in shading. One can go there with no fear of being thought vaguely Papist-inclined or, on the other hand, vaguely Holy Roller. It is dignified; it is spiritual without excess; it is, though of course entirely unwittingly so, the perfect place for a national politician who may be concerned to reflect so far as is humanly possible the authentic norms of his place and time.

Now, whether Eisenhower was deeply "religious" was obviously his own exclusive affair, and there is no intention here to make impertinent speculations upon the point. It is fair to say, however, that there *were* times when his membership in the National Presbyterian Church of Washington did not seem to bear too heavily upon him. Nor did he ever pretend to the slightest bent of piety, though he had men around him, notably Ezra Taft Benson, his Secretary of Agriculture, who had the habit—and the entirely sincere one—of audibly praying in Cabinet meetings. If certain sophisticates made sport of this, the country did not—and neither did Dwight Eisenhower.

To the contrary, his personal philosophy was strongly that of to each his own, and his political philosophy was in some ways not much different. One of the ironies of his time was that his appointments to the Supreme Court, notably that of Earl Warren of California as Chief Justice, created what was by any measure the most liberal court in history to confront a neoconservative President, who would surely have been far happier had the Court turned out to be far less activist. When in 1954 the Court handed down its historic decision holding school segregation to be both unconstitutional and publicly immoral, Eisenhower found himself in one of his very few real quandaries.

Inevitably he was tirelessly pressed, in press conferences and elsewhere, to comment upon this decision. Resolutely, and sometimes wearily, he refused, standing upon the principle that it was not his function either to agree or to disagree with an independent arm of the Federal Government. His critics saw this as a moral evasion of the duties of Presidential leadership, and a good many of them suspected that his motives were less a great reverence for the separation-of-powers doctrine than a lively disinclination to offend an American South which had been very good to him at the polls. Still, he stood his ground steadfastly—and again, in the end, nobody much was really very angry after a while.

His close human connections with the Southerners of the Senate—who are traditionally powerful in military affairs and thus had always been friendly with him—never prevented him from offering the toughest civil rights proposals ever, to that time, put before Congress, though here, too, he bowed on occasion to what he believed to be genuinely impressive Southern objections to certain legislative details. Nor did these connections stay his hand when, for the first time since Reconstruction, he acted as President to send Federal troops to the South —to Little Rock, Arkansas, to put down a civil rights rebellion by the state authorities.

Still, on the whole harsh topic of civil rights, Eisenhower's basic position was that one could not legislate racial fairness, that it really had to come, as so often he said, "from the hearts of men." This homily was much sneered at, again on the incorrect assumption that this was only his way of staying out of the line of fire. But it has not fared so badly in history, at that. His real concern here, as elsewhere, was to avoid a national polarization on the issue, and in his own way he showed a striking courage in dealing with it.

He was openly and genuinely contemptuous of political appeals to race or class, and he made none whatever himself. Indeed, his candor was sometimes striking. During the 1960 campaign of Richard Nixon, Eisenhower was at length persuaded to hold a pseudo conference, strictly partisan in motivation, with a group of Republican women who had been carefully assembled for the purpose. One of them was a black woman from Louisiana (who would certainly in a subsequent national climate have been waved away as an Aunt Thomasina), and when her turn came she asked the President the expected questions about his civil rights achievements.

He was standing alone at a mocked-up fireplace; his questioners were seated below him. Glancing at the woman from Louisiana, he began his reply by saying, "Now, you people . . ." It was plain that he was drawing a line of differentiation between *those* people and *his* people, but it was also plain that there was no malignant discrimination intended. Nobody was in the least offended, though an eminent Republican acquaintance of mine shuddered and muttered, "Godamighty! If Dick Nixon had said that in that way, church would be out for sure." The gaff was simply vintage Eisenhower.

How he got along with minority groups was illustrated strikingly in his own campaign for re-election in 1956. Looking back into the returns one could find the most patent of evidence that he scored impressively over Adlai Stevenson precisely where one would have supposed he could not—among blacks and labor in general. This made no sense on its face, for Stevenson was far the more liberal, and far more articulately so. Eisenhower himself was inclined to put this down, rather grandly, to what he considered his own "soundness" and Stevenson's "unsoundness" on what the President habitually called "national security issues"—meaning foreign and military policy. Maybe so. But one doubts it, and the more so because a Republican professional disposed of the question at the time with this observation: "Nuts. 'National security issues' my foot. Those fellows just like and trust Ike." It is perhaps as good an estimate as any.

Still, whatever may be the right of it as to these precise voting groups, there is no doubt that his mastery of "national security issues" was always his strongest point, particularly with the powers-that-be in American society, as represented by the so-called Eastern Establishment. His very nearly unbelievable virtuoso performance was his coming to power from a military background and making this a virtue instead of what it had always been—a considerable vice.

In his time in office he followed a seemingly casual and zigzag course which made this country's military power simply unchallengeable, in his era at least, and at the same time persistently kept down, in the Pentagon and out of it, those excessively martial spirits who wanted him to lift any ceiling whatever on military expenditure. The generals and the admirals, who had at some times and in some circumstances seemed slightly held in awe by a former artillery captain called Harry Truman, got brisk treatment indeed from General-President Dwight Eisenhower. In truth, he never did wear much of a West Point school tie, even though with a sensible-sized drink or two of an evening he could on occasion be sentimental about old alma mater. In consequence the country got, early on, the correct impression that he was one of the *good* generals and, for that matter, a real general no longer in any case.

Juxtapose him on a social occasion with Omar Bradley or Maxwell Taylor, say, and one caught the distinction right away. If it would be too much to say that Dwight Eisenhower's mother had never raised her boy to be a soldier, it could certainly be said that she had never raised him either to martial gallantry as a way of life or to the form of martial risk-taking that is vital in a field commander and inappropriate in a President.

Thus when, only with infinite reluctance and infinite care and calculation, he committed his Presidency and thus his nation to any course of manifest danger in world affairs, he had the country twice with him: once because people implicitly trusted his "military know-how," and again because of his powerful strain of prudence and forbearance. There was, of course, in Eisenhower's "public image"—in the present context a largely self-created one—something of what in street language is called corn. But it was legitimate corn; it only added a certain surface appeal to a perfectly genuine thing.

For in politics there is in practice what might be called a legitimate kind and degree of demagoguery, as there is in all life. The great trick, as every Responsible has known consciously and as Eisenhower himself seemed to apprehend by a sort of osmosis, is to distinguish between the legitimate and harmless and the illegitimate and irresponsible kind.

In any event, the Eisenhower "image" in foreign and military policy was an extraordinarily skillful blend of strength in restraint and resolute readiness to defend truly basic national interest without ever issuing alarmist cries. Viewed in a superficial light it had a certain small but discernible touch of Papa Knows Best. And while this was annoying to many who were concerned with Presidential "style," it was nevertheless hard not to acknowledge in the end that Papa *did* nearly every time Know Best, after all. For what Papa really did was to allow, if not indeed to help create, the development of an aura of great "toughness" in international affairs about his Secretary of State, John Foster Dulles, while Papa himself was habitually seen as hovering in quiet decisiveness in the background with far less belligerent posture and purpose.

Thus it was that while this nation's allies in Western Europe were almost constantly in pain at what they believed to be Foster Dulles's Calvinistically extreme views of the menace of international Communism, they were nevertheless as constantly reassured by the overriding presence of the figure of Dwight Eisenhower. If he was a father figure to the Americans, he was even more so to the Europeans.

Dulles early on proclaimed the doctrine of "massive retaliation." That is, he bespoke an American readiness to loose the atomic weapon without hesitation against any wide Soviet military thrust in Europe or elsewhere. Dulles, moreover, was more than once heard to say that the world's neutral nations were "immoral" nations in their refusal to take up an open position of hostility to Communist expansionism.

Now all this was heated rhetoric to the bulk of the Europeans, most of whom were understandably concerned to shun any talk of even the possibility of atomic warfare over their terrain. Still, back of Foster Dulles there was always "Ike"; Ike would see to it that his principal minister did not go too far.

Because of this notion, which was widely held abroad but not here at home, since on this matter the European heads of state were far better informed than was general American public opinion, there grew up two mutually exclusive understandings of the Eisenhower-Dulles relationship. The important fellows abroad believed, and rightly so, that Eisenhower was invariably the boss in any showdown. Many intellectuals and foreign-policy activists here at home believed that Eisenhower was only a sort of relaxed Constitutional monarch and that Dulles was not simply Eisenhower's principal minister but actually his boss. They could not have been more wrong, though Eisenhower characteristically did little to correct the misapprehension.

Thus when, in 1956, as the American Presidential election campaign was reaching its climax, Eisenhower broke with the British, the French and the Israelis and condemned their invasion of Nasser's Egypt, sophisticated American opinion supposed him to have been led by the nose by Dulles. The truth is that this was Eisenhower's decision from first to last—not because he underestimated the moral justice of this attempt to break Nasser's noose about the Suez Canal and not because he failed to grasp the growing intimacy of Nasser's Egypt with the Soviet Union. Eisenhower reacted strongly, and in private even angrily, against this adventure in part because he *knew* it could not succeed militarily, so chaotically inept was Britain's planning for the action, even apart from Britain's total lack of effective liaison with the only military force then of real value to the enterprise, that of Israel. Secondarily, he was moved by his awareness that the Allied case here simply would not go down politically in the United Nations. Finally, he was deeply annoyed with the then British Prime Minister, Anthony Eden, for what the White House considered a disposition to hide things from Washington.

Eisenhower was so annoyed, in fact, that his private communications to Eden during the crisis period sharply turned from his customary "Dear Anthony" approach to the glacial salutation "Dear Mr. Prime Minister." A man who intimately participated in this affair from the official American side once told me that every significant American *démarche* and response in this business was not only written out by Eisenhower personally but also handed to Dulles with brisk instructions that this and no other was to be the language employed.

To be sure, when Eisenhower directed the United States to join the Soviet Union in the United Nations in hazing the British, the French and the Israelis, the effect was to throw the traditional Anglo-American relationship into a deep chill that was profoundly regrettable. (Once, years later, interviewing British Prime Minister Harold Macmillan, an old and good "Ike" friend, I found him absolutely unwilling, even in private, to say a single word about "Suez.") But the alternative to Eisenhower's policy, as one can see a good deal more clearly now than one could then, might actually have been a nuclear exchange with the Russians, who were boldly threatening to send their rockets to England and might actually have done it.

More precisely, however, Eisenhower's conduct in this affair was the most luminously clear illustration in all his years in power of his approach to international crisis. He knew that the British-French-Israeli sortie was lost before it began; he never believed in fighting actions only to lose them, unless the issue involved was literally one of American life or death. He knew, too, that the West could not confront the Soviet Union here with any assurance that a third world war might not ensue. Finally, he knew, or at least strongly suspected, that there could be a way out of this mess—as in a different context there had been out of the Korean dilemma—that while surely not ideal could at least be tolerable.

At any rate, the action he took here was Eisen-howeresque; one finessed one's way through inadmissible forms of danger wherever what was at stake was not mortally unnegotiable. One also, of course, went to a total commitment when the issue was transcendental. Since while Suez was ablaze he was up for re-election (but feeling no great urgency one way or another), there was, again, some suspicion that he had taken the line he took for domestic political reasons. He had, so the indictment ran, long presented himself as a "peace" President; so here he was avoiding a showdown in order to preserve this picture of himself intact. But again it was a case of a skepticism more facile than sound.

For he told an associate at the time that he would "lose a hundred elections" before he would alter his course. And, however naïve this may sound, he meant it. After all, moreover, had he really had a domestic political motive here he could scarcely have failed to take into account the probability that the so-called "Jewish vote" would not care very much for his position. Of course, what came out of it all was an even bigger landslide than that of 1952—and nowhere bigger than in urban areas of high Jewish population.

At the time I was working for the *New York Times*, attempting to sense national political feeling, and as it happened I was, at the moment of the invasion, down in Dallas speaking in my hotel room to Senator Lyndon B. Johnson of Texas. I had asked him to have his political people make an estimate of how Texas would go in the election. He had just handed me a slip of paper summarizing their views, and the conclusion actually—and surprisingly to me—favored Adlai Stevenson over Eisenhower. When the flash came over the radio that the invasion was under way, Johnson leaned forward and said, "Let me have that paper, please." He took it and tore it up and threw the tatters onto the floor. "It's all over now," he said. "Eisenhower landslide."

A "peace" President Eisenhower had certainly been here. But a "peace" President he never was on any occasion where he judged that vital national interest required vital national risk. The Eisenhower who had gone so softly with Colonel Nasser in the Suez crisis of 1956 (because Nasser, though a menace, was not an insupportable one) unhesitatingly flung American Marines into Lebanon in 1958 to halt a gathering Nasser *Putsch* which threatened not simply an international waterway but rather a whole anti-Communist Middle East position. And this he did without apology—and without asking Congress what it thought of the business, in spite of all his tireless deference to Congress on other matters.

Again, the approach was different, but the essential philosophy was the same, in the gathering storm in French Indochina that led at length to the partition of Vietnam and, finally, to the war in Vietnam. He never committed American combat forces to South Vietnam, but only because the drama of conquest had not in his time proceeded to the point where the peril was unarguable or where the presence of American troops would have been *militarily* wise. He did, however, commence the basic American commitment to the integrity of South Vietnam, and in all the years that followed he never apologized for or in any way disclaimed the fact that philosophically he was the father of the American intervention, which at length he handed over to John F. Kennedy.

Actually, in his post-Presidential years he upheld Kennedy in Vietnam as later he would uphold Lyndon Johnson, upheld them so faithfully and so generously as to establish a legend of unsurpassed magnanimity from an old politician to the new ones. For the notion that he was not much of a "fighter" was perhaps the greatest of all the oversimplifications about him. He was simply not a foolish or a theatrical fighter. He was, instead, the best and most effective kind of "fighter" there is—a fighter who never lightly entered a contest or foolishly leapt before looking and who never lost one that indispensably mattered to his nation, if not to himself.

Some of his associates, and notably Foster Dulles, bore mortal troubles with striking bravery; Dulles all but crawled to work in his last months of life until ravaging cancer made it literally impossible for him even to stand up again. Eisenhower's own repeatedly serious illnesses he carried with no derring-do, for derring-do was not in him, but only with a subdued impatience at the disorderliness of it all; very much, actually, as he looked at uninformed criticisms. When, rarely, he replied to these, his manner was more one of mild irritation than of anger or outrage. To endless suggestions that he had overorganized the White House into too rigid a staff system, one reminiscent, it was said, of the Army, he observed finally, in his memoirs, that he was astonished by "contentions which seem to suggest that smooth organization guarantees that nothing is happening, whereas ferment and disorder indicate progress."

Still, in eight years in the White House he was really hard and widely hit on only one occasion, and this involved an episode of a high melodrama which was quintessentially foreign to his nature. Just as, in May 1960, he was preparing to meet Nikita Khrushchev in a Summit Conference in Paris there came the embarrassing disclosure that the Russians had brought down a high-flying American U-2 "spy plane," which had been conducting lofty surveillance over Russian territory. This sort of surveillance had been made necessary to American security by the prior refusal of the Soviets to accept Eisenhower's notably generous proposals for "open sky" arrangements by which each side could know what the other was doing.

Still the timing of the U-2 incident was unfortunate—not to mention the fact that the Russians had captured not only the aircraft but also the pilot, and had us, as the saying goes, dead to rights on the issue of espionage. Unfortunate, too, was the collateral circumstance that the Washington Government was caught out in a series of evasions in its initial responses. Now, of course, no one but the excessively naïve can really suppose that any great power is going to tell the truth, the whole truth and nothing but the truth about its intelligence operations. All the same, a great deal of public hope for the projected Eisenhower-Khrushchev talks had been pumped up, and the Russians now drew themselves up in righteous indignation and torpedoed the Summit Conference before it could begin. Those American politicians and commentators who had long been urging more "flexible" American-Soviet exchanges were bitterly angry, and for the first and last time in his tenure Eisenhower was driven into something approaching a defensive position.

He met the issue by deciding to go to the country via radio and television; to accept sole responsibility for the U-2 missions and to point out, without any great beating of drums, that it was, after all, possible that the Russians had found here a mere pretext for avoiding a meaningful Summit that they might at all events have decided to avoid in one way or another. Whether he was extraordinarily perceptive or only very lucky here, there *were*, in fact, a good many subsequent intelligence straws suggesting that the Soviets had, indeed, had second thoughts about Paris and would not in any case have allowed the conference to proceed to any useful conclusion.

In any event, the central point in the whole affair was that the storm in domestic opinion soon passed over, leaving Eisenhower quite unharmed, solely and simply because the American people trusted him. This sense of affection and trust remained with him to the end when, in the early afternoon of March 28, 1969, he died in his seventy-ninth year, in Walter Reed Army Hospital, peacefully and on a bright early-spring day.

What then ensued was a manifestation without precedent in this country's history. The passing of a man who by that time had been out of power for nearly a decade was treated as a national deprivation like no other. It was not a case of aching national grief, as it had been for the young John Kennedy so brutally slain. Rather it was a mood of mellow elegy for the incomparably fitting end

—in quiet, in peace—of an elder statesman who was a kind of beloved uncle to this country. The eulogies by President Nixon and by former Presidents Harry Truman and Lyndon Johnson dwelt not so much on the greatness of the man who had gone as they did on the simple virtues of his life—"honor, courage, integrity," as Johnson put it; goodness, as Richard Nixon put it.

Nixon recalled what had not beforehand been known —that just before he finally lost consciousness and death arrived, Eisenhower had said to his wife, Mamie, "I've always loved my wife. I've always loved my children, I've always loved my grandchildren, and I've always loved my country."

This was his own epitaph, and this was the epitaph in the minds of those who mourned him. To be sure, harsh realism might suggest that his time of power was a simpler time than the times that followed and that in the late sixties his approach to political leadership might, indeed, have been inadequate to the endless social and political alienations with which in an enfevered nation his successors had to cope. Still the great test of it all is in the doing of it all; and when Eisenhower himself had to do it, he did it very well indeed. He had not only loved his country; he had driven a sickness of bitter divisiveness from it. And, most of all, he had protected it without bravura but also with the undemonstrative courage that had come, as he himself had once said he had come, "from the heart of America."

· · ·

BOOK FIVE

John F. Kennedy

• • •

John Fitzgerald Kennedy's lot was to be superficially the most widely known and in substantial fact the least understood American President of the twentieth century, if not, indeed, of all our history. His assassination in Dallas on a bright November day in 1963 ended a political career of the utmost improbability, considering that this man had reached the Presidency before his forty-fourth birthday and, in doing so, had breached an old and subtle but terribly real barrier against the elevation of any Roman Catholic to the highest office of a nation founded by Protestants. But the tragedy of Dallas (whose agency was misrepresented from the beginning and may, in truth, be misunderstood to the end) opened an era of legend-making such as this nation had never known, not even in the aftermath of the murder of Abraham Lincoln.

For the man who killed John Kennedy, Lee Harvey Oswald—and was himself subsequently murdered by a nightclub operator who had been a fanatic admirer of the

President—had had some degree of indoctrination in both the Soviet Union and Castro's Cuba. To the extent, therefore, that Oswald could have been said to have any political orientation, it was plainly of the far left and certainly not the far right. All the same, the echoes of the fatal shots had hardly ceased before excited radio and television reporters had assured the world that the slain President had been victim of a right-wing plot in a notoriously right-wing city. The conclusion had been leapt to because in Dallas a handful of hysterical matrons had, some time before, spat upon Ambassador Adlai Stevenson, and no doubt because in Dallas there was a certain number of undeniably ultraconservative oil multimillionaires.

It was a case where all the facts in the world and all the prestigious and objective inquiries of a high bipartisan commission headed by the liberal Chief Justice of the United States, Earl Warren, were never wholly to overtake and never wholly to lay to rest a malignant myth spawned by the irresponsibility of what is called "electronic journalism."

Never had a whole city (and in this instance a whole state, a state that had been carried, and not lost, by Kennedy in the 1960 election) been so slandered with so little recourse. Still, there it was. Elementary reason and fairness toward the city of Dallas and toward the home state of the successor President, Lyndon Johnson, were for a time wholly lost, swamped by the awfulness of the assassination itself. And elementary reason and fairness are not to this day fully available to that city and that state; and certainly not in Europe, which is in any case historically prone to the conspiratorial interpretation of any and all acts of violence directed at a head of state. Putting aside reason either in uncontrollable grief and anger or in their search for the quick money that accrues to sensationalism, a few men opened a long and macabre campaign to impeach the findings of the Warren Commission, findings vouched for by the Kennedy family itself, because the Warren Commission had found it impossible to unearth a right-wing plot that never existed.

Thus were the facts of John Kennedy's death put under the duress of ugly fiction and into a prison of untruth. And for quite opposite motives, motives of grief and decency, the facts of his life and career were molded into a mural of unreality.

For the nation and the world long mourned, and to a high degree still mourn, a man who never was; a kind of politician who never existed; a statesman celebrated for qualities he never had, and thus denied the qualities that he really had.

The truths that have survived him are not negligible in number, but they ill describe the John Kennedy who actually was. Greatly gallant was John Kennedy? Yes, he was. A figure of charm and grace? Indeed, he was.

He was a man of extraordinary physical and moral courage. It was the courage of a skinny stripling of an ensign in the Second World War swimming three miles in a dark sea with one of his crewmen from a shattered PT boat in tow; the courage of an adult man who lived half his life in intense pain.

A leader, an expositor and a creative innovator in liberal thought? This he never was, and both his times and the national circumstances neither required this of him nor would those times and those circumstances have been well served thereby. A powerfully *successful* popularity-poll (as distinguished from a properly functioning) President he never was. The fact is that just before his life had drawn with such horror to so premature an end, John Kennedy himself knew that he might be facing in another November, the November of 1964, that popular repudiation that had come to Responsibles before him and would come to others when he had gone.

For perhaps the outstanding of all his intellectual traits was a self-candor and an habitual and unafraid confrontation with objective reality equaled by one other politician known to me, and one alone. This, ironically, is the man Kennedy defeated in 1960 for the Presidency, Richard Nixon. Indeed, Kennedy had gone to Dallas primarily to seek, along with his Vice-President, Lyndon Johnson, some means, somehow, to bring some order into the affairs of the Democratic party in that highly critical state against the onset of the 1964 Presidential campaign. For about Kennedy, as well he knew and as he had plainly said to friends, even then the shrill eagles of dissent and opposition were gathering.

The most experienced politicians in his administration shared John Kennedy's own characteristically wry view that for 1964 the omens were ominous ones. Why? Why, simply because, as had been the case with Harry Truman and would later be the case with Lyndon Johnson, Kennedy had resolutely spent most of his capital of facile acceptability by attending with single-minded devotion to his ultimate duty to be President of the United

States of America and by letting the lesser politics of it all look pretty much after itself. And, as nearly always, the lesser politics had, of course, really not been looking after itself very well.

For what had happened to John Kennedy was simply this: Having entered office with a superb academic understanding of the Presidential institution, the great burden of its actualities had at length descended crushingly upon him. Kennedy had learned, in short, that in contemporary America the Presidency is much harsher even than that "splendid misery" which Thomas Jefferson had termed it in an incomparably less testing time. He had learned that when all was said and done his true mission was both singular and singularly unrewarding in a national atmosphere which sought most of all comfort and ease and domestic self-indulgence. His hard task was to protect the vital interests of a nation in emotional flight from the implications of the exercise of world power in a globe of unending danger and crisis.

The cheering, for John F. Kennedy, had long since stopped when the rifle bullets in Dallas brought an end to a life he had lived in a skeptical, active fatalism. This fatalism was the force that impelled him to enter the Presidential lists prematurely by all past standards and thus to evoke the sour comment in 1960 from old Harry Truman that young Jack was "not ready" and ought in common sense and good manners to wait a few more years. Indeed, a consciousness of the inevitability of death, not in some comfortably distant time but perhaps in some very near time, was an almost constant spiritual companion to this man of so much outward gaiety and so much quiet inner resignation.

Asked by a friend at a dinner party in the home of Arthur Krock in the spring of 1960 why he thought he should "go for broke" so early, Kennedy took this somewhat impertinent inquiry with complete good humor and even with a kind of amiability, much as to say, "I'm glad you asked that question." He looked bemused for an instant and then replied, "Well, you see, it is not good to wait around for anything in this life." Then, conscious perhaps that he had been on the gloomy side at a convivial table, he put in this addendum, "Anyhow, here is the situation. I am a member of the United States Senate, right? Well, no use kidding around about it, you can't really be a good Senator and be always running for President. I am running for President now—and I am not a good Senator now, and I know it. So I am making the run right now, to reduce the time of not being a good Senator to the irreducible minimum. The point is that I'm not going to go on running. I'll make it now, or not at all."

He paused then in clear apology for his solemnity, for he never liked to bring a serious note into any social gathering. Surely one of the shyest politicians of all time, he was very shy here, and so he launched at once into a risqué and self-deprecatory anecdote to make restitution for what he had done.

He even threw in a remarkably plain four-letter word or two, for this was very much a young man of his time, and genteelly "correct" deportment or language was very far from his habit. So, indeed, very far from his true metier was the aura of the patron of the arts, the lover of advanced music, the fond follower of, say, Pablo Casals, that was later carefully thrown about him by staff associates who irked him even while he felt kindly toward their intentions. And there was, strangely enough, at the same time a degree of humility in him toward those he considered more precisely "intellectual" than himself. If, therefore, he ostensibly gave more leeway to White House intellectuals such as Arthur Schlesinger, Jr., than he should have done, this was the reason. He had thought of himself as undistinguished at Harvard, and in a way he suffered the odd and wholly undeserved sense of lack found in many truly superior people before those who are overtly and professionally scholarly.

This trait sometimes made it appear, though in fact quite wrongly, that faced with an authentic intellectual he felt himself at a disadvantage and thus was inclined to pay more heed than he should have paid to what that intellectual recommended to him. So marked was this impression among the more sensitive of the President's well-wishers that one of them once took up the matter with the late Supreme Court Justice Felix Frankfurter. "I don't quite understand what's the matter with Jack," the Justice replied. "God knows, I appreciate the life of the mind and all that, but isn't he carrying this thing a bit too far?"

"Perhaps," said the friend. "Perhaps he overvalues purely academic distinction because he never quite had it himself. Why don't you, Felix, as the very doyen of academic intellectuals, the Pope, so to speak, of the church of the high brain, go to the President and give him a sort of papal blessing of reassurance in this business?"

"Ah, yes," said Frankfurter, greatly amused. "Maybe I will, maybe I will. Anyhow, let's face it, academic distinction is fine, but I have never known many academics who could carry an aldermanic ward in an election, let alone a country." But, of course, Frankfurter never really went on this improbable mission of Presidential reassurance. And, of course, it never was necessary anyhow. For while Kennedy's attitude toward intellectuals *was* at times slightly awed on the surface, his real attitude was by no means self-abasing.

A personal anecdote is in point here. About midway in his term I had sought one of those usual off-the-record interviews. The President, who himself had briefly served as a journalist, always held a lively interest in the craft and in its people. He greeted me in kindly fashion but very soon turned an admonishing eye upon me. "Why," he said, "do you go on persecuting my professors, and particularly Arthur? I know that you are not anti-brains."

"No, Mr. President," I replied, in some discomfiture. "And I'm not really persecuting Arthur, say, as Arthur. But I am bound to say that I really do think some of his ideas, both on public policy and on politics, are not wise —and I understand he has a great deal of influence with you." Kennedy grinned widely, with the pleased, gamin touch that was one of his charms, and responded, "No, no, you've got it damn well all wrong."

"Arthur," he went on, "works over *there*"—pointing to the East Wing of the White House, which commonly shelters staff of importance but not staff actually engaged in policy-making. These latter fellows traditionally sit in the West Wing, near to the private office of the President. "Arthur is a *writer*—and a good one, too, don't you agree?" I said I did. "And anyhow," said Kennedy, "I owe a great deal to Arthur. He made me respectable among the intellectuals." By this he meant that Schlesinger, an old backer of Adlai Stevenson, had "switched" before the 1960 Democratic National Convention and gone over to the Kennedy side.

This, in truth, was a not inconsiderable thing. For though it is widely forgotten now, John Kennedy always identified his real antagonists in intraparty Democratic power struggles as "the Stevenson people." He was far more comfortable, though this, too, has never been generally known, with "the Johnson people," as in fact he was humanly and personally far closer to such supposedly benighted Southern Senators as Richard Russell of Georgia and John McClellan of Arkansas than to such as Senators Joseph Clark of Pennsylvania and Wayne Morse of Oregon, both of whom set his teeth on edge.

And Kennedy's instinct in all this was entirely sound. He never had from his traditional and proper Republican opposition—right and proper in a two-party system —nearly so much bitter criticism as he had from the left wing of his own party. These he called "the ADA-ers" —meaning members of Americans for Democratic Action. He would never join ADA, though ironically his brother, the late Senator Robert Kennedy, was at length to make ADA people his principal allies. This attitude was partly a matter of personal temperament, for

Kennedy detested what he called "weepers," meaning reform-oriented politicians who in his view spoke too loudly and too glibly of race and other problems. He had as little to do with them personally as his office and his responsibilities would permit.

Nor was he in the slightest degree unaware, as his life was drawing to a close in 1963, that what has now become the pacifist and essentially anti-Federal-power New Left was moving in upon him for his refusal to abandon his commitment to South Vietnam and was, indeed, proposing his destruction. What he did not and could not know, of course, was that the in-party assault being readied for him would in time strike in fullest force at his successor, Lyndon Johnson.

As for his interest in the arts, the common picture of the Kennedy White House as a kind of perpetual salon for the pursuit of the true excellence in the higher arts was not gladly suffered by him. It was not, of course, that he was "against art," as he might have put it. It was simply that he had a healthy distaste for what came to be called "The Beautiful People." He recoiled from pretentiousness in any form. Genuinely civilized, he was never arty. A good reader and a sensitively educated man, he saw no cause for a public celebration of these attributes. And he could not bear anything which, using the patois of ordinary people as he preferred to use it in private conversation, he felt to be "phony." And most of all the soirée interpretation of his White House troubled him. He vaguely felt toward the end that in social and even political terms a circle was closing about him. Always sensible of the fact that he began as a minority President

—and very much one in geographical terms, since his mandate had for all practical purposes ended well east of the Mississippi River—he was perturbed, and so told me, by what he feared was a growing public impression that the White House had become the true home only of the Eastern seaboard fragment of the nation.

Still, of course, he had no time to do anything about it and perhaps would not have done anything about it in any case. Like all Presidents he was discovering that the White House was, as he put it, "a bad place to make new friends," and so he held on to the old, though sometimes his eyes held a clear glint of private amusement. He was at heart, even more than most Presidents, in some senses and at some times a man very much alone, not only in his office but also in his life.

Again like nearly all the Responsibles of our politics, his sense of ultimate personal privacy was very strong and the highest of his gaiety had always in it a strain of profound, though never "weeping," melancholy. He was the true skeptic in a profession whose atmosphere is not unduly hospitable to overt skepticism. At bottom he was, however odd this may sound, far more a classic conservative than a liberal of any stripe we have known in recent years. And here is a fact which has become incredibly clouded by fiction in current history's interpretation of Kennedy.

For his lasting contribution to this country was never in his domestic programs, the most important of which were hardly allowed to get off the ground in a remarkably reluctant Congress, nor yet in his presumed appeal to youth. It was something very different indeed. What

John Kennedy did for his country—that country which in his Inaugural address he asked all to give to rather than to take from—was to give to it a sense of its essential unity, if only it would grasp that unity, and an awareness, if imperfect, of its obligations to a larger world which was more than "the Free World," though this, too, was a vital part of his concern.

Even before he had been sworn in, in January 1961, amidst an appalling blizzard which had made Washington a field of ice strewn with the debris of stalled automobiles, he had privately seen his mission as far more one of consolidating a country than of "breaking new ground," to use a cliché widely current at the time. Asked by a friend whether he intended to be a "liberal" or a "conservative" President, he replied with sharp impatience and with a grimace of distaste for the simplism of the inquiry, "Neither. I hope, instead, to be a *responsible* President."

This did not mean, of course, that he was concerned only with not rocking the national boat or some such nonsense. No, it was very far from that. It *did* mean, however, that he had reckoned up his mandate from the election with completely unemotional objectivity, seeing it not only for its glory but also for its sparse narrowness, and that he had far more interest in the hope that history might call him Kennedy the Just than Kennedy the Reformer. From the beginning to the end of his political career, indeed, both his actions and his speech were characterized most of all by a philosophic integrity—"integrity" in its connotation of oneness and of true consistency.

As a young member of the House of Representatives from a classical Irish constituency in Boston, he took from the outset, for illustration, an attitude in many respects wholly untypical, considering his political origin and circumstances. Appointed to the House Labor Committee at a time when the newly victorious Republicans of the Eightieth Congress were setting out with blood in their nostrils not merely to regulate but to punish labor, his service was a model of quiet distinction, for a freshman, and certainly a model of independent thought. The labor leaders had automatically counted upon him, as by definition a liberal Democrat arising from a liberal and inevitably pro-labor-machine district, to join their lamentations that whatever the ultimate act of Congress it must surely be "a slave labor act."

But young Jack Kennedy, sitting so quietly at the very end of the committee table as the most junior member of its minority side, was not at all prepared to oblige. Most of his Democratic colleagues on that side of the table knew what was expected of them and had no difficulty at all in delivering the goods. Kennedy apologetically but firmly demurred. With utter deference to his Congressional seniors and elders, and with a faintly smiling and faintly challenging face toward the labor barons who appeared before the committee as witnesses, he begged leave, over and over, to differ from them all.

Was it not just possible, he asked, that the country really did need some additional legislation? Would anything at all that might be done really and automatically be a "slave labor act"? Really, he thought not.

The long and short of it was that he brought to the

committee's steamy—and often seamy—deliberations a kind of objective judgment rarely seen there, and never shown by any other Congressional freshman of that time. To say that he made a great personal mark upon the ultimately ensuing Taft-Hartley law would stretch a point. But that he bravely resisted the emotional excesses of the labor skates, in Congress and in the unions alike, was beyond doubt.

All his political life, that is to say, he had distrusted automatically "liberal" or "conservative" solutions. And he went into the White House with this posture unchanged. There was, for one example, a vast gulf between the actuality of his approach, as President, to the running sore of race relations and civil rights in general and the approach that would later be generally attributed to him. In truth, he was most gingerly about this question, having a historically oriented view of skepticism toward the possibility of quick and total solutions to vast, encrusted social problems of whatever kind. It was not at all that he lacked a sense of social or racial justice; it was not at all that he held any kind of brief for racial discrimination or was in any way simply "afraid" to come to grips with it in the White House.

Still, as again in all his political life, he had no trust in solutions offered at the top of the voice and absolutely no stomach for those who offered them. Along with this he had an irreverently lively suspicion of "howlers" in the field of civil rights, rightly seeing that some of them were far more interested in exploiting this issue for political gain at home, among minority-group and urban constituencies, than in doing anything substantial about the

matter. This had been unforgettably borne in upon him
during his days in the Senate. Here, as in the House in
the days of labor legislation, he had refused to perform
as expected and in consequence had suffered serious
damage to his "image" among the more advanced liberals of the Adlai Stevenson–Eleanor Roosevelt school.

The position in the Senate was this: A Democratic-
Republican coalition, led then by Majority Leader Lyndon Johnson, was preparing what became the Civil
Rights Act of 1957. It was far from perfect, of course, but
it was still the best obtainable act of that time, and notably so in its genuine steps toward Negro enfranchise-
ment in the then obdurate South. The heart of the sanc-
tion being proposed here was to empower the Federal
courts to enforce equal rights, especially in suffrage, by
holding in criminal contempt those Southern election
functionaries who discriminated on the ground of race.

As the struggle went forward there unfolded a classic
illustration of the central reality that the Senate's long
inaction in civil rights had been in fact quite as much due
to the all-or-nothing demands of the extreme civil rights
forces as to the well-publicized obstructionism of the
Southern filibuster. At last this point was reached: It was
clear that the Act could be brought off (and it should be
stressed here that for all its shortcomings it was, indeed,
to be the first really substantial progress in this field
since Reconstruction) only if the Senate was prepared to
stipulate that offending Southern registrars brought to
the bar of the courts should be granted the traditional
right to a trial by jury rather than by judge alone. This
was, on any dispassionate reading, no improper conces-

sion to "Southern Bourbons." It was a mere extension of the elementary right of any defendant facing criminal charges to be tried by his peers. Historically, it stood upon the precedent of labor's right to jury trial long before granted by Congress to union leaders brought to book in the old days of the "yellow dog" court injunctions against strikes.

Still, the more vehement liberals bitterly fought this provision and sought with skill and passion to make the issue the very litmus-paper test of who was and who was not truly interested in broadening the Negro franchise in the South. Now, here was Senator John Kennedy, already clearly a future aspirant for the Presidency in light of the strong showing for the Democratic Vice-Presidential nomination which in the preceeding year he had only very narrowly lost to Senator Estes Kefauver of Tennessee, facing his moment of truth. By every visible standard, he simply *had* to stand here with the ultraliberals, for the simple reason that if he was ever to be nominated for President it strongly appeared that he could reach that goal only with the tolerance, if not the total support, of the Northern and urban liberal forces. Yet he knew perfectly well that the real issue here was whether the Senate of the United States was or was not going to enact a good, if again an inevitably imperfect, civil rights bill. He did not hesitate; he cast his vote for the right of jury trial.

That he could never emerge unhurt in sheer political terms from this decision he, of course, knew very well. Far-more than his prior omission to vote on a Senate censure of the late Senator Joseph McCarthy, this action made him powerful critics, and some outright enemies, among liberal Democrats in the power centers of the North. The reason was that the McCarthy abstention, while certainly very far from Kennedy's finest hour, was to a degree both forgivable and not damaging to the essential purpose. After all, McCarthy was finished in any case, and that was the aim of the exercise. Moreover, Kennedy was flat on his back with major illness at the time of the critical vote (though, of course, he still could have made his position known, illness or not). Finally, it was a fact of life that much of McCarthy's more emotional support was from other Irish Catholics—and this was what John Kennedy was, too.

The jury-trial thing hotly pursued Kennedy in all the preconvention maneuvering leading to his nomination and election in 1960. It is, for example, most likely, though of course one cannot say it for certain, that this was the real sticking point with Mrs. Eleanor Roosevelt, FDR's widow, in her opposition to Kennedy before the convention. That lady (and her influence was great) had taken a dim view of Jack Kennedy's going back to his first race for the Senate in Massachusetts. She had brought against him an accusation, which he repeatedly and vainly asked her to retract, that his father, tough and rich old Joseph Kennedy, was spending far too much money on young Jack's political march upward. John Kennedy himself was much more hurt by this than he ever indicated in public, nor was he really forgiving in private. At last, he adopted a policy of waving it all away with jokes. He had, he once observed dryly, just received a wire from "generous Daddy" in which "Daddy" had said: "Dear Jack: Don't buy a single vote more than is necessary. I'll be damned if I'm going to pay for a landslide."

The truth is, parenthetically, that John Kennedy had never had much time for the Roosevelt family, not excluding Franklin D. Roosevelt; and, being himself, he never really pretended otherwise. Perhaps influenced by the bad blood that had arisen between FDR and Old Joe, who served for a time as Roosevelt's ambassador to Britain and managed to become a blazing isolationist, Jack Kennedy could, as he put it, "take the Roosevelts or leave them alone very easily." While writing a memoir on Roosevelt I asked Kennedy, who was then President, for the nature of his recollections on that day of mighty tragedy when Roosevelt died, and received a reply that was contained, indeed: "I am afraid that at that time I had no deeply traumatic experience at all."

The point here (and it bears endless repetition in light of the posthumous legend of a John Kennedy as the loved and loving perfect knight of the extreme liberal activists of his party) is that at no time was he really at home in his political life with that form of liberalism—and was never, until after his death, really acceptable to it. Not in the House of Representatives, not in the Senate, not in the Presidency, and not for that matter in all those power struggles within the Democratic party in which he took part was he ever truly the first choice of most of the very same advanced liberals who have most vocally mourned him in death.

What he really was, throughout, was a mildly liberal working politician, deeply sensitive to and actively seeking that political "consensus" in public affairs which in the time of his successor, Lyndon Johnson, became a bad word to the academically oriented liberal community. In his real person, in fact, he was, in the usual definition of a highly fluid term, considerably more conservative than Johnson or Harry Truman, either.

Though he disliked large, pompous words such as "commitment," the fact is that he did have a commitment for change but only for slow and carefully worked out change. He had far less audacity in running to greet the new than did Johnson. It has been forgotten now, but when Kennedy was seeking the Presidential nomination of 1960 the authentically "liberal" adversary was Senator Hubert Humphrey of Minnesota, who later became Johnson's Vice-President. This was clearly evident everywhere, but never more unarguably plain—at the time—than in the Kennedy-Humphrey Democratic primary test in West Virginia. Any who might care to go back and read the campaign utterances of these two contestants would find that it was Humphrey who took the populist line and Kennedy who took a far more reserved line on such issues as poverty and welfare in general.

To put the case in transatlantic comparative terms, Kennedy was infinitely closer to, say, a British Prime Minister Harold Macmillan than to a Prime Minister Harold Wilson, whereas the reality was the other way round as to such other Democrats as Johnson, Truman, and Humphrey—and, yes, Franklin Roosevelt, too. For John Kennedy, at the very end of it all, shared the core of what is philosophic conservatism. This is in secular terms as previously noted as to Churchill, what might be called a conviction of Original Sin; a lively dubiety toward the doctrine of man's undoubted, or even likely, perfectibility.

Thus it was only with great wariness that he approached the more liberal concepts of most of his White House associates. Though "pragmatism," too, has become a disliked term to all those associates in the posthumous years, the years of the legend built by men unconsciously and humanly remaking him in their own preferred images, no single word could more exactly describe the actualities of this young and martyred President. He believed in much, but he also doubted much, as so intellectually realistic a biographer as Theodore Sorensen, the man who was actually the "closest" to John Kennedy in his lifetime, has recalled while all about him others were writing biographies of a man who never was.

For Kennedy personally spent a great deal more time and effort in seeking honorable common ground with his conservative friends in Congress, and notably in the Senate, than one would ever dream in reading most of the memoirs of his era. It was not by any accident that perhaps the favorite of all his phrases, and the most used, was the dry phrase, "The *fact* of the matter is . . ."

It was the fact of the matter which most genuinely and even with a certain private passion he pursued. It was the fact of the matter and the promise of *performance* and *achievement* in any and all of his designs, as distinguished from the splendidly rhetorical visions of the unattainably perfect order and of the perfect and impossible state which were the goals of many of those around him. At the very bottom of it all, this is a partial explanation of why it was that his tenure was rich, on the whole, in authentic foreign-policy successes and rather barren, when examined dispassionately, in domestic successes.

For as to domestic policy, he faced what Grover Cleveland once called a condition and not a theory; and the condition was essentially intractable. His failure to carry large geographic areas of the country in 1960 meant that, in terms both of their rank and file and of their Congressional representation, even when Democratic representation, they had either rejected him outright or put him upon a kind of chill and unbelieving probation. He had foreseen this in its general outlines, if not in all its stony specifics, at the same Democratic National Convention at Los Angeles that had nominated him over the real challenge of Lyndon Johnson, over the secondary challenge of Senator Stuart Symington of Missouri, and over the emotionally satisfying but never real challenge of "the Stevenson people" in behalf of Adlai Stevenson.

The nomination itself had been brought off by very hard, very acute and very open manipulations that were neither unlawful nor untraditional except in the high degree of their highly public toughness. Kennedy had been put over, at the end, by a powerful combination of urban, Catholic bosses, beginning in New York and spreading westward beyond Mayor Richard Daley's now-storied Chicago. The nature of the victory was from the start a matter of lively concern to John Kennedy. He was fully aware that the aura of big-city, Irish-Catholic politics roughly and plainly at work must be of a special sensitivity to him, as he was certainly an Irish-Catholic aspirant and, in appearance but not in fact, also a product of the urban-machine version of American political life.

All this, he knew, was bad "image" stuff to the South, some of which he knew he simply must have to win election, and everywhere in the country to the rural-Protestant ethos which he was, of course, inevitably challenging. Masses of "inside" stuff have been written about Kennedy's consequent decision to ask the powerful Senate leader, Johnson, to go on the ticket as the Vice-Presidential nominee. Some of it is substantially true; some of it is simply the enfevered stuff of which enfevered political conventions are all too full.

"The fact of the matter" was this: Kennedy not only wanted to win in November, but he also held both a profound and a profoundly decent desire to win election in a tolerably united party and to appeal, both for the election and for the future, to an electorate justified in thinking him to be a man of moderation and a man interested in the nation's common future beyond the election returns. He and Johnson had had a bruising fight in the early maneuvering at Los Angeles, and with lesser men the human divisions between them would have become irreparable. But there never was a time when Kennedy, once he put his hand to politics, was lacking in adulthood.

Before Los Angeles, he had said, to me among others, that by purely objective criteria Johnson was the ablest man in sight for the Presidency, though he had added to this judgment another to the effect that Johnson could not, however, win in November in any case. Johnson, who had become an active candidate only late in the game, did not spare the horses when in fact he entered. He broadly suggested that the country needed to lead it "a man with a little gray in his hair." He had taken sharp thrusts at Old Joe Kennedy's isolationist record and at his undoubtedly bad standing in the books of most of the minority groups of the country. And he had hit John Kennedy hard for his failure to be recorded, one way or the other, on the great test of "McCarthyism."

Kennedy, as the man to beat for the nomination, had retorted in softer terms but nevertheless in terms not precisely endearing to his adversary. But now, when the nomination had been sealed, all this was rightly forgotten, Kennedy and Johnson both being true pros in a hard trade. So Kennedy went to Johnson and in substance said this: "If you don't go onto this ticket it is going to lose and you are going to be to blame and I am going to say so." Johnson, of course, submitted. To suppose, as many have done, that he had deliberately angled for the job, it is necessary first to suppose that he did not know the frustrating emptiness of the Vice-Presidential office and that he was unaware of the all-too-obvious fact that a Senate majority leader is to a Vice-President in real and here-and-now power terms about as is, say, a chairman of a large corporation to its sales manager.

Thus Johnson, a Protestant of old American stock, a rancher by avocation, a Southern-based liberal of distinct populist undertones, became one of the decisive elements, if not *the* element, in Kennedy's victory in November. But the accommodation was not at the outset and would never be, in the longer run, either popular or tolerable to many of Kennedy's people, most notably including his brother Robert. Nor, ironically, was it to the very groups, such as ADA, whose objective interests were most of all actually served. The reason was that these fellows supposed, as John Kennedy did not, that Johnson was simply a rustic relic of Southern feudalism bereft of all the requisite liberalism.

To them, John Kennedy's choice of Johnson was a surrender to what they would later term "the Senate Establishment." To Kennedy it was, in fact, the reverse; and he was somewhat distantly amused at all the clamor from the Left. These people never grasped that they had wholly misunderstood Johnson in terms of his political and ideological interests. And they never understood, in the faintest way, the actual personal relationship that existed between John Kennedy and Lyndon Johnson. Kennedy knew his man because he had served with him in the Senate, in a relatively lowly place to be sure. In the Senate they had been friends, not enemies, and not even rivals until the onset of the 1960 Presidential year. Moreover, they shared a common contempt, though never so harshly expressed by either in public, toward what Johnson called the always-talking-never-doing liberals and what Kennedy called "the bleeders." They looked at the ultimate realities of politics very much in the same way—and both had already had their fill of visceral liberal hostility, which annoyed them almost as much for its irrationality as for the fact that they were its targets.

Moreover, Kennedy had regarded Johnson's convention attacks upon him as within the rules of the game as they both understood it, whereas he never quite forgave Adlai Stevenson's form of political competition at Los Angeles. In behalf of Stevenson, perhaps without his prior knowledge but certainly not without his subsequent consent, there assembled, in and about the convention hall, the first truly massive congeries of political hippies that American politics had known. Kennedy thought, then and later, that the Stevensonites were hitting below the belt, whereas Johnson and Stuart Symington were being no nastier than the form allowed.

Now, to understand all this one must first accept the fact that Kennedy's substantial political training had come in the arena of the Senate, which has its own special code of what is permissible and what is not. Stevenson never knew that place. The done and the not-done things there are not describable in precise terms; but the Senate types know very well what they are. For an illustration or two: A certain demagoguery is acceptable there, of course, but it is not playing the game to practice it beyond a certain degree. A good Senate man must not, for example, speak or act in obvious and unarguable detriment to objective and nonparty national interest, just as he must not exult with shrillness in his victories nor lament aloud in his defeats. Kennedy considered that Stevenson's people at Los Angeles had driven whole cloudbursts of impermissible "bleeding" through this evanescent but nevertheless very real fabric of the "done" thing, and, indeed, that Adlai Stevenson, particularly by his refusal to second a Kennedy nomination when it became inevitable, had played the game very poorly himself.

It would be quite wrong to say that Kennedy as President carried this sense of distaste and disappointment forever next to his heart. But it is entirely true, to my personal knowledge, that he was never happy around Stevenson (whom in fact also he never understood) and never really wanted Stevenson in his administration. He had told me in confidence, before his inauguration and even before he was nominated, "Everybody is saying that Adlai will be my Secretary of State. Everybody is wrong. He won't be in my Cabinet at all." The upshot was that he made Stevenson his ambassador to the United Nations, believing he simply had to go this far to placate "the Stevenson people." But there never was from first to last any really comfortable human association between these two.

Now, of course, Los Angeles and the convention and all that really could not have been the sole reason, for Kennedy's personality was free of vengefulness and vindictiveness. My own reading, based upon the circumstance of happening to have been in Kennedy's confidence in the matter and happening also to like them both very well was that a simple matter of human chemistry was involved in all this.

Kennedy was highly intuitive, both as a person and as a President, and to him there was always in Adlai Stevenson something of the unfortunate Dr. Fell. The Kennedy who was seeking the Presidency had thought that not only "the Stevenson people" but also Adlai personally were running a precious kind of game. The Kennedy who was President most strongly felt that Adlai Stevenson flinched not merely from any notion of power wrongly or oppressively used but actually from the mere fact of power itself.

This was not in fact the case, but the suspicion was inevitably and repeatedly fed by the circumstance that Stevenson's writ was to talk up "peace" at almost any price among a majority at the United Nations that was tirelessly suspicious of the motives of the colossus America. And Stevenson's duty, in those occasions when he sat in on foreign crisis sessions in the White House, was to be primarily a Cassandra toward any project implying the possibility of the commitment of American military force. He had the hard onus of the Devil's Advocate—and almost any other Devil's Advocate would have found in John Kennedy a less annoyed listener.

At all events, the most urgent "talent search" of the whole countryside could hardly have found for Kennedy such totally divergent associates as Lyndon Johnson and Adlai Stevenson. Kennedy felt that if Johnson had been rough as a political adversary, it was the roughness of a worthy adversary and, importantly, also of an adversary who at some point had stood some chance of winning. Not so, of course, with Stevenson.

Too, the alliance struck up at Los Angeles between Kennedy and Johnson (Johnson called it a case of "Austin to Boston") was not only highly fruitful in the 1960 election but generally prospered, all accounts to the contrary, thereafter. Kennedy told a caller at his Georgetown residence even before his inauguration, "Any fellow who thinks he is going to make points with me by biting at Lyndon Johnson has got a hole in the head." It was in a spirit of enlightened magnanimity on Kennedy's part and of enlightened loyalty on Johnson's part that they went on together. Each man considered the other to be far from perfect, and there was never any political love affair between them. Kennedy was a good deal like a young lieutenant out of West Point who has a tough and able top sergeant in his company and takes a sensible satisfaction from it.

Johnson, on his side, was carefully and even mammothly correct in the relationship, doing what was asked of him by the President to the best of his ability, but never intruding, either politically or socially.

In a word, neither was a cream puff in the relationship —and each was maturely glad that this was so. Kennedy's basically mordant sense of humor at the situation was often tickled, even while his compassion for a man of great savvy stuck off in the Vice-President's office was entirely genuine. He was sensitive to the inherent frustrations of the Vice-Presidency, particularly in the tenancy of a man so long accustomed to excercising great power personally and urgently in the alma mater of both, the United States Senate. But Kennedy also was tough-minded, and he took, at times, a half-affectionate, half-sardonic attitude toward Johnson's plight. Once it was reported that he suffered from a thing called Addison's disease; the President told this to me with a chuckle and added, "God, I'll bet old Lyndon is reading up on everything he can find about Addison's disease."

Still, in serious terms, the President was often disturbed, and sometimes profanely so, by recurring "rumors," put about by anti-Johnson elements, sometimes from within Kennedy's own entourage, that Lyndon

Johnson was to be "dumped" as Vice-President in 1964. Kennedy could poke fun at and with Johnson, but he knew the vast difference between joking in good heart and joking with the bite of malice in it. Moreover, he and Johnson were members of a special club. So much was this the case that at critical times Kennedy, a far abler man at protecting his personal flanks than was Johnson, went out of his way to protect his Vice-President from unjustified criticism or from any responsibility that really had not been shared by Johnson for anything that went wrong in the administration's planning and actions.

He went out of his way, for one illustration, to exculpate Johnson from any connection whatever (as indeed there was none, for Johnson was absent from Washington at the time of decision) with the first great failure of the administration. This was the ill-timed and ill-done Bay of Pigs invasion of Castro's Cuba. "Leave Lyndon right out of this one," the President once observed to me. "He was in on neither the take-off nor the crash landing."

Those who peddled "dump Johnson" rumors sometimes elicited from Kennedy an ugly four-letter word beginning with the letter "s." For he could talk very toughly.

When, for example, he had got into bitter contention with the steel industry by trying to force it not to raise prices, the rumor got about that he had remarked in anger, "My father always told me that businessmen were sons of bitches." To a White House caller he recalled this report and then said with the broadest of smiles, "Who on earth could believe that I, John Kennedy, would ever really say that these sons of bitches were sons of bitches?"

Of course, he never meant this literally. He was only relieving himself momentarily of one of his oldest frustrations and senses of personal injustice. This was the circumstance that from first to last the business community generally never really quite trusted him because of its irrational conviction that he was at heart antibusiness and fatally resolved to spend far too much public money. He was never the one and he never intended the other; it was again a case of a public misapprehension of his actual spending views, which were, in fact, more conservative than otherwise.

Of course, he had only to look to some of his own assistants to find the source of this misapprehension. But while one side of him knew quite well where the source really was, he never moved frontally or harshly against it. In part this was simply because of the well-established habit of White House walls to draw ever inward upon the chief occupant. In part it was because Kennedy, like Truman and Johnson, practiced a kind of personal loyalty that was not wise. I, for one, have always believed that had he lived and been re-elected in 1964, some changes would have been made. But this, of course, is the sheerest of speculation.

As with all Presidents it was early and with impersonal brutality borne in upon him that while the holder of that office held vast and occasionally even unwelcome power in one sense, in another sense all was vanity. It is easy for a President to lay out and to proclaim a policy, no matter how high and frightening its implications. But it is sometimes hard—so huge, so intractable, so sullenly uncooperative is the very nature, sometimes, of the great bureaucratic beast upon which in the end he must ride —for a President to put that policy into effective motion and keep it there. Bureaucracy's term for this purpose is "implementation," and the very sound and texture of that word is illuminating. For it connotes a turgid poverty of expression, a stiff upper-clerk mind's notion of decorum and propriety along with a high sense of the wisdom of playing everything safe and a strong inclination toward letting many problems sink gently into a limbo lying somewhere between the "in" and the "out" baskets.

But if keeping the bureaucracy in motion and on the right track is a difficult job, surpassingly more difficult is that of dealing at all with the lesser priorities of the Presidency. The man at the top simply hasn't got either the time or the strength, once he has somehow coped in a day holding only twenty-four hours with all that he simply *must* do, to turn then to putting into good order the relatively minor affairs and problems of his House. That Kennedy had and retained advisers who were doing him no good, not because they were maliciously inclined but simply because they were never really in his own intellectual pattern of effort and aim or even within his own ideological lodge, is beyond question. He had a good complement of "bleeders" and "weepers," men of the best motives and the poorest capacity to help forward what was actually the generally centrist design of his administration. Some of these misunderstood the nature of his mandate in the beginning and miscalculated his intentions to the end. Thus in many instances they unintentionally misrepresented what he was doing while alive and misreported those actions after he was dead.

Yet, he clung to them, in part because of personal affection and perhaps in larger part simply because the problem was not and could not be at or even near the top of his priorities. All modern Presidents, at least, and oddly and particularly all strong and active Presidents, have lived with this dilemma. In Kennedy's case, however, it was an abnormally sharp one, because of experience he never had. He came to the Presidency with far less schooling than average in the techniques of executive leadership. Truman, Johnson and Roosevelt, for example, had been through that mill pretty well in one way or another before taking the oath in front of the Presidential shield. All of them had had a strong foretaste of the inertia that is inherent in both the so-called "policy-making" branches of the administrative service and in that strange apparatus known as the Civil Service. All this was substantially unknown ground to John Kennedy. As a member of Congress he had dealt only with staffs that were small, flexible and manifestly devoted to his person and career and thus quickly responsive to his orders and his personality.

So it was that in sitting at the very top of the towering and sometimes tottering Federal pyramid he inescapably met more than his fair and in-built quota of frustrations, just as he did in Congress for other reasons. The bureaucracy really accepts no master in any case, and it scarcely knew this particular master at all. Nothing, not even active malice in others, so long as it was clever malice, ever offended Kennedy quite so much as sheer, irrational and insensitive incompetence and/or mulishness for its own sake. In point of fact, his interest in the purely domestic governmental departments—Commerce, Agriculture, Labor—was tentative and fugitive at best. At the minimum it was simply nonexistent. Thus, his Cabinet meetings were on the whole arid in interest. And when it came to the routine of most of the departments his attitude was about like that, say, of a professional writer called upon to examine the splendid intricacies of an IBM computer or to throw himself heartily into a long discussion of the freight-rate differential between North and South.

His approach to the "farm problem" is a good example. As always, he was in private engagingly open about this personal reality, though this never meant, of course, that he lacked concern for the country's agricultural economy or for its people. Once, a visitor, finding the President wrestling in his White House office with a proposed message to Congress on farm relief, was welcomed if only because of the relief he brought. "Me dealing with the farm problem—my God!" said Kennedy, in tones of weary self-deprecation.

So in practice he really rode personal herd only on two Cabinet departments—State and Defense, and State far the more. Startled foreign-service desk officers never lost their sense of bemused wonder to find the President either physically or by telephone at their elbows to inquire urgently and impatiently about this or that situation or area. The unalterable routines and the sacred "channels" of the State Department were challenges at which he repeatedly flung himself. About them he often had the air of a man saying to himself, "By God, I'll master you yet." Nor did departmental rhetoric, the cant of the foreign-service trade, ever escape his outraged respect for logic, for order and for plain English. Against this latter he inveighed vigorously among his private friends and also within the foreign-service club itself.

Finding him so engaged, an acquaintance once sought to lighten the atmosphere by recalling that his problems here were not unique to himself. Franklin Roosevelt, Kennedy was informed, once learned that in the wartime blackout the civil-defense authorities had posted in stores and so on the admonition that "illumination must be extinguished when premises are not in use." Shaking his head over this, Roosevelt had thundered, "Damn it, what they mean is: Put out the lights when you leave!" Kennedy was entranced: "Ah, yes," he said, "that's it; that's it."

His inability really to command the bureaucracy did not, however, ever prevent him from dominating those very fields in which his administration was a success—foreign and military policy—while he was most of the time losing the game up on Capitol Hill.

Here his difficulty was complex in the extreme, and he never was able wholly to surmount it—in the area of domestic legislation, that is. To begin with, he had never been in or near the true centers of Congressional power, either in the House or in the Senate. In both places, to be sure, he was liked; in neither was he held in the slightest disrespect. Still, a good many things worked against him. There was the storied thinness of his Presidential victory, the blackout of his candidacy substantially everywhere save in Eastern Kennedy Country and Southern Johnson Country. There was, at the beginning at least, still the so-called "Catholic Issue." This made him sometimes unduly reticent and even timid toward pushing social legislation, such as Federal assistance to the schools, which inescapably involved either the actuality or the strained possibility of collision with the doctrine of separation of church and state. The same factors simultaneously enfeebled or at least inhibited some of his Catholic Congressional supporters from the degree of backing they might otherwise have given him.

And then there was, in both houses of Congress, a disposition among the elder movers and shakers to regard the Kennedy administration as on a long probation. This was not in hostility, as such, but simply in a vague feeling that here was an innovation—"very young fellow, Jack Kennedy is; will need quite a bit of seasoning" —that might not be around very long. Just as the alleged importance of religious bigotry has been much overstated in the Kennedy campaign for the Presidency, any estimate that Kennedy as President was punished in Congress for his Catholicism would be utter nonsense. All the same, the surface social aura of his administration (and, to repeat, an aura he himself never made) was far from helpful to his domestic designs.

For it appeared to many, and importantly to some Congressional power centers which were wholly free of any kind of bigotry, that the White House had become some madly gay "in" place for an excessive pursuit of a jet type of culture which was inhospitable to, if not actually alien to, the common culture of a wide country.

Kennedy never lacked good, tough and productive liaison agents with Congress; these were quite as useful as all the circumstances could permit. Still Kennedy, though he made genuine advances in Congress on some subjects, was never able there really to break through on the highest national issues like civil rights, public education and public medicine. If he could have gone to Congress himself on a working and day-by-day basis, it may be that all would have been different. But the great fact that he was really Kennedy the Unknown there, on many days and in many ways, was a negative factor of the most capital significance.

Moreover, and no less important, there was the hard fact that very few IOUs to him were ever outstanding on Capitol Hill. Of course, he had never been a member of a leadership core which puts the common run of members under obligations of both a personal and a political nature. Nobody in Congress was much in debt to him, either for past help or favors given by him or for his assistance on election day. For since he barely squeaked through in November of 1960, his candidacy had certainly had no helpful coattail effect upon Congressional candidates of his party. More nearly, the reverse was true.

Too, if his Presidential mandate was somewhat equivocal, so, too, had his own personal power position always been. Both as a member of the House and later of the Senate he was in a way an outsider, because simply as a human being he never faithfully reflected the Irish-

Catholic constituency from which in the literal and surface sense he had sprung. There never was a time in the
Massachusetts days when he lacked a good deal of tolerance, if not also a good deal of private support, from
patrician Yankee-Republican and totally Anglo-Saxon-
Protestant sources. Still, what he gained here—and it
was not accidental, for in all his political career, he
sought to avoid polarization in *any* of its forms—inevitably cost him not the ballot-box support of the "Irish,"
which was, of course, automatic, but at least any total
hero's identification with them. As President, as before,
he knew this quite well.

In 1960 the very model of the Beacon Hill Republican
aristocrats, Senator Leverett Saltonstall, to his quietly
mannered pain found that the luck of the draw had not
only put him up for re-election in a basically Democratic
state with a man named Kennedy running for President
but also that another man called Kennedy was running
for the Senate. This was fickle fate at its unkindest; and
"Salty," as Kennedy called him sometimes, was hard
pressed and sorely laden. Because I felt that Leverett
Saltonstall's old-fashioned private and public honor simply required his re-election, whatever his shortcomings
as a political leader, I wrote a piece saluting him somewhat for what he had done in the Senate but mostly for
the way in which he had done it. Now, of course, this
was a moment when his own most urgent interests
clearly required Kennedy to regard as black heresy any
suggestion from anywhere that it was a sound idea to
vote for any Republican. Thus when I next met the
Democratic candidate for President of the United States

there was a natural supposition that he might well feel a bit cool toward this business of promoting Leverett Saltonstall. But not at all.

Surrounded at the moment by some of the most faithful of his Democratic partisans, Kennedy vocally chided me, with a gleam in his eye, for siding with his party enemies. But when I left the gathering he walked to the door with me and, jabbing me with a brisk and jocular elbow, he said, "How can you ever, ever be forgiven for doing this dreadful thing; what the hell has mere objectivity got to do with anything?" In short, he was highly pleased. He never lifted a hand in that campaign to hurt Salty, just as later on he only wiggled a reluctant partisan finger or two in what was really mock assistance to Democratic efforts to defeat the Republican Senate leader, Everett McKinley Dirksen, in Illinois. Dirksen, of course, had opposed Kennedy with a true-blue partisan heart—on domestic matters. But in those grand and fateful foreign issues, issues which Kennedy like all the other Responsibles always held to be quite beyond party politics, Dirksen had been to Kennedy a gallant friend and ally.

Kennedy would no more have done anything seriously to injure Dirksen, notwithstanding the dogma of a pseudo-religious constancy to any and all "liberal" Democrats as opposed to any and all bad "conservatives," which was clung to by some of his White House Palace Guard, than he would have moved to destroy, say, Lyndon Johnson. For Kennedy knew what was finally and inescapably the real name of the game in the Presidency. He knew that giving all respect and deference and honest compassion to all the nation's huge and hard domestic problems, and taking no whit away from the manifest urgency of any and all of them, he lived in a situation of relative needs and of relative crises. He knew that while it was vital to work for racial justice and urban renewal, it was *transcendentally* vital to protect and to advance the power of this nation in a world which in the most literal sense had no other decent great power to which to look.

He knew, for illustration, that the presence of offensive Soviet missiles in Castro's Cuba within ninety miles of the American coastline was so immense and so brooding a reality as to dwarf every reality here at home. He knew, no one better, that his fund of operating influence in Congress was limited by all the circumstances that have been described here and that it must be most carefully husbanded by him. For on the mortal topics at the top of his agenda he most desperately required at best the assistance and at worst the reasonably benign neutralism of the Everett Dirksens and of the Southern conservatives of the Senate and House. He could never sustain this if he pushed these fellows too hard on domestic issues. For no matter how many might wish that it was not so, the fact remained that the power centers in Congress were in control of just such men and would continue so to be. Joseph and Rose Kennedy had raised in this man no happy dreamer, as he himself would sometimes remark to those about him who constantly pressed him to "take on the Establishment."

So he did *not* open hopelessly foredoomed Crimean charges against the power centers—not even on civil rights—but rather used such force as he actually had toward what was in fact his highest necessity. This was the necessity to conduct a prudently firm foreign policy with the irreplaceable help of those in Congress whose enchantment with the domestic New Frontier was at the best of times far less than ardent.

And this he did, humanly preferring most of his ostensible ideological enemies to many of those who were ostensibly his co-ideologues. And this is why he became and remained a Responsible. This is why it is possible to salute him in good conscience as a great President, but not with a mind paralyzed by too much grief too long held and teeming with posthumous images of a man who never was. He was a President who failed in much but succeeded in much that was incomparably higher. He lost many battles, but he won all the wars of great decision—except, perhaps, the war for his right and proper place in history.

A rationalist, in him rationalism triumphed; a pragmatist, in him pragmatism never lost place to mere good intentions. A charmer, he was much more than that, and little concerned with that; to him charm was sometimes a tool of his trade, but never any more than that, and often not even that.

For the controlling fact of all was that John Kennedy saw himself as primarily committed to lead a historic evolution in this nation's foreign policies in such a way as to preserve the central principle of Communist containment of the Truman-Eisenhower years with a less simplified and overtly "hard" line than the former artillery captain had used and yet with more readiness to contemplate power showdowns, if need be, than the former Commander in Chief of Allied Forces in Europe had shown.

Kennedy, to be sure, saw the world in a more bookish way than had either of these predecessors. It was bookish in the sense that he had a more academically educated mind than Truman and a far more formal awareness of history than Eisenhower. But the critical point so often missed in the years after his death was that Kennedy also never, at any point, supposed that national power was in itself an evil thing or that as Commander in Chief he could rightly refuse to invoke power when and as its exercise was patently necessary to the national interest. Where a much earlier predecessor, Theodore Roosevelt, had recommended speaking softly but carrying a big stick, John Kennedy shunned slogans with distaste, but he never for a moment forgot or flinched from the awesome leadership obligations that were no less real for him.

Not only was foreign policy his specialty by the stark demands of his Presidential position; foreign policy had been his favorite political subject in all his career. It is surely probable, to put the thing no higher, that his decision to seek promotion from the House to the Senate was heavily influenced by the reality that the House has truthfully very little to do with foreign affairs, whereas the Senate can have very much to do with them. As a youngster whose father was Ambassador to London, Kennedy had written his first book on the subject, a book called *While England Slept,* and in his relatively brief career in the Senate his real interests had been in the foreign-policy direction. To be sure, he had, like all Senators, to perform many routine chores in the service of his constituents. He could, for example, rival the best of them in the New England delegation in speaking up earnestly for, say, finished textiles and in deploring the occasional wintertime shortages of fuel oil along the upper Eastern coast. He did the things he had to do and did them well. But he also did them with a certain amused light in the eye; and he was always grateful when he could put some job of this sort off on Theodore Sorensen or some other member of his staff.

Ironically, indeed, John F. Kennedy, for all his youth and glamour and surface modernity, was in the real sense about as close an approach as one could have found to the old-fashioned Senator who considered his real writ to be national and who regarded a certain deference to the mundane problems of his state as slightly painful, even if clearly necessary. He sat at the very bottom of the table on the Foreign Relations Committee, but he never lacked a full appreciation of what was going on there and why.

What he did in the domestic field in the Senate, in short, he did with his left hand. With his right hand he grappled with the great complex of world affairs. And all this he did—and the point is an important one—with absolutely no automatic acceptance of anybody's stereotypes. Officially and in the shorthand sense a liberal, for illustration, he privately rejected the whole liberal foreign-policy establishment of the time by reaching the conclusion that General of the Army Douglas MacArthur had been more nearly right than wrong in wishing greatly to expand the American military commitment—

and, of course, the American military risk—in Korea and into China's sphere.

Again, he broke with the Establishment, and indeed with practically every other important Democratic politician from Harry Truman down, in his view that the Republicans of the early postwar years had something of a point in arguing that Democratic administrations had let down Nationalist China under Chiang Kai-shek. These two positions were very far out for a Northern Democrat (and in this writer's opinion were both wrong, for that matter). They are presented here—and will surprise many people—simply to show that John F. Kennedy's foreign-policy interest from the start was real, skeptical and tough.

The only vital attribute he lacked at the beginning of his Presidency was that of experience, and this he gained. His Vienna meeting early in the game with Nikita Khrushchev was never the disaster for Kennedy or the West which it was proclaimed to be by the very critics who later all but canonized the President in death. It did not show the new President to be incapable of dealing with that enormously skillful Russian; it did, however, begin the new President's education in the vast difference between a theoretical and a working knowledge of the cold war.

For if Khrushchev approached Kennedy as a mere stripling and a tyro, Khrushchev left Vienna with a very different impression of his vis-à-vis. Kennedy himself had matured in a matter of days.

The learning process for him, however, came to full and bitter flower only in the immediate aftermath of the disaster of the ill-planned and ill-favored Bay of Pigs invasion of Castro's Cuba in 1961. The purpose was, of course, to uproot a Communist lodgment; the end of it was a humiliating failure for an enterprise which gave Cuban counterrevolutionaries too much encouragement, too little help and far too much subsequent disillusionment and bitterness. The tale has been told and retold. The obvious net of it was that Kennedy should either have stayed out of it altogether or gone in with whatever it might take in American military power to bring it off.

And yet in the longer reaches of history this essentially tragic episode had the greatest of value, if harsh it was, to Kennedy himself and to the United States of America. For in it, from it and because of it he became in deepest fact a *President*. It was a frightful tutorship, but it was worth all that it had cost. By fortuitous circumstance I spent some two hours with President Kennedy at his Virginia country place, Glen Ora, on the weekend that brought the final blows in the collapse of this broken sortie into Castro's Cuba.

Kennedy, looking so very young, wore tennis shoes, chino pants and a sweat shirt, and we had a memorable conversation at the edge of his swimming pool, while Mrs. Kennedy was going about in a pony trap with her small daughter, Caroline. The President was deeply disconsolate as he compulsively discussed and rediscussed what had happened in the Bay of Pigs. No decent writer discloses certain kinds of private conversations with any President without his consent; in this case I had this consent. Nor does any decent writer purport to give some total stenographic transcript of a talk of this kind. The substance of it, however, was about this:

Kennedy began by sadly remarking that while he believed he had long understood the nature of the American Presidency in an academic way, only now did he understand it in fact. There were unshed tears in his eyes as he talked of the casualties from this undertaking, and these tears changed to glints of anger as he mentioned his belief that he had been terribly let down by advisers in the Pentagon and in the Central Intelligence Agency. He talked both in anguish and at random, and I did not interrupt except as and when his manner seemed to invite interruption. Slowly, in this way, it emerged that his chief complaint against the Joint Chiefs of Staff was that they had not advised him in so many words not to undertake the action at all. "But Mr. President," I said, "surely that would have been well beyond their function. Wasn't *their* function only to put all the military prospects and strengths and weaknesses before you, so that you alone could finally say yes or no?"

"Yes," he replied, "yes, I suppose that really is the right of it. You are saying that the responsibility is mine alone, aren't you?" It was poignantly plain that in his inexperience and in his instinctive deference to high military rank he had, in fact, forgotten the unique, the unsharable, burden of ultimate decision which perforce he bore as Commander in Chief. He went on then to discuss what should be done to pick up the pieces, both in substantive foreign-policy terms and in domestic political terms.

He toyed for a moment with the notion of having a

major investigation, to find who had failed or erred and where. But then, straightening his back (which, as nearly always, was paining him), he threw a pebble into the swimming pool and said loudly, "No, no; no investigation. Historically and constitutionally, I am it; no matter who made what mistakes, they are all *my* mistakes in the end. That is the meaning of the system; that, after all, is how it is." (I have used sparse direct quotations here; but those I have used are engraved in my memory and I can vouch for their accuracy.)

He went back to Washington from Glen Ora to announce that he and he alone was responsible for the Bay of Pigs; never again did he allow any question to arise as to where the onus of failure must and would lie. He did, however, later cause a head or two to fall, notably that of Richard Bissell of the Central Intelligence Agency. This was ironic—and none knew it better than Kennedy —but there was not a shadow of petty motive in it. It was ironic because it was Bissell, of all people, who had truly grasped the nettle of the Bay of Pigs and who had, from the beginning, bravely spoken out for the necessity of the use of American air power.

But Kennedy knew things about leadership that are hard but also true. One of these was that while he had formally taken the full blame for Cuba, public opinion in a free society positively demanded some scapegoat; nobody could fire the President but the President on his side simply had to fire somebody. The then head of the CIA, Allen Dulles, was both too big and too Republican and was, moreover, a brother of the former Secretary of State, John Foster Dulles. So Bissell had to walk the plank. It was not an easy decision for President Kennedy, but only theorists can suppose that he could have avoided it.

Still, it was the grim consequences and lessons of the Bay of Pigs that enabled Kennedy in the following year to come to grips with his greatest crisis—and splendidly to win through. This was his "eyeball-to-eyeball" (the phrase was that of Secretary of State Dean Rusk) confrontation with the Russians upon the discovery that they had not merely infiltrated Cuba by way of Castro but had also placed offensive missiles there. This was where his Presidency came fully of age; and this, too, was where the first major rupture with his far-liberal constituency was opened up.

For in standing firmly in 1962 where he had wavered in 1961 John Kennedy took the great and irrevocable decision to be a "strong" President in the one area where it really counts—foreign policy. All this led with logical inevitability to the second great decision, which was to commit American combat troops to South Vietnam's resistance to internal and external Communist aggression. It is true, of course, that the massive commitment, the far larger "escalation," was to come under the subsequent Johnson administration. But all this is in the philosophic and high policy senses a matter of detail. The fact of the commitment was the heart of the matter, as the acceptance of this vast and terrible—and absolutely necessary—risk was the central glory of the Presidency of John Fitzgerald Kennedy.

Had he lived it is probable, if not utterly certain, that the bitter fallout would have burned him, as later it

burned Lyndon Johnson. In any event, no greater disser-
vice to the memory of John Kennedy has ever been done
than was done in the subsequent efforts of some of his old
associates to suggest that he would have run from the
struggle in Vietnam when the casualty lists lengthened
and the opposition grew and grew.

If the attempted salvation of Southeast Asia, in the
bleak and infinitely larger necessity not to allow the
Chinese Communist version of open aggression in the
Cold War to be vindicated in Vietnam, was Kennedy's
finest and most bittersweet hour, his diplomatic successes as to Europe were his most glowing one. I am well
and truly aware—bruised and aware one might say—
that to call Vietnam a great and right Kennedy decision
will be "unpopular," as that war itself long since became.
All the same, an action is not wrong or unwise simply
because it does not, or is not allowed, to succeed; is not
"immoral" merely because an unprecedented wave of
propaganda has long since so said. Presidents cannot run
the grand affairs of this nation on Gallup polls or even
"popularity," as before this I have tried to show. Let each
man have his own view; for myself I am not one of those
who have "changed"—not one of those, in short, who
spoke yesterday in one vein and today in another.

At any rate, no President in this century—save perhaps Franklin Roosevelt, and even Roosevelt only in far
different circumstances—made so great and so construc-
tive a mark upon European opinion. And here again lay
one of the grand paradoxes of Kennedy's tenure. Precisely those qualities and images of his White House aura
which had inhibited him domestically in the American

Congress—the impressions of a too flippant gaiety, of a somewhat continental social tone—were his greatest recommendations among Western Europeans.

For the root fact is that John Kennedy was not merely the first Catholic President of the United States; he was the first also to reflect something other than the Anglo-Protestant ethos that had dominated the White House in all the generations that had gone before him. In a subtle cultural sense Kennedy was the first "European" to reach the zenith of American power. (Of course, some of the British sometimes regard themselves as "European," but the Europeans do not.) Frenchmen, Italians, Belgians, Germans, even if always vaguely, sometimes unconsciously or even merely glandularly, saw him as the human embodiment of something fine and new (and also very old) at the top of the American power structure.

And so did many in Central and South America—and many, indeed, who were themselves ex-Catholic and professionally anticlerical.

So it was that he was able to sustain a form of subcultural, emotional, not necessarily entirely rational but nevertheless useful communication with Europe—something that no other American President had ever done. His, in these terms, was a strange politics indeed. He could and did engage the deepest of European loyalties and command the deepest of European fondness not so much for what he did as for what he was or, in some cases, only seen to be. At heart, of course, he was as "American" as it is possible to be, and in the best meaning of that term. But countless millions abroad saw in him a shining something, a glittering triumph of a new man who was all the same the heir to much that is old.

Thus, when he went, for illustration, to a Berlin newly besieged when the notorious "Wall" was rising in glowering meance and said there in his half-New England, half-continental voice that he was "ein Berliner," he was apprehended to be speaking a spiritual truth that had no concern with mere literal exactitude.

And so it was that when he died, he died, in the old phrase, as almost truly "a citizen of the world."

Perhaps the last irony was that in his life he had wanted most of all not the leaping, pulsating, squealing, uncritical fondness of the many, whether here or abroad, but rather the cool, even, aware appreciation of the comparative few who lived where he himself really lived; that is, in a personal house of reason, of detachment, of ironic humor, and of sound and courageous but never emotionalized devotion to his country and his people.

. . .

BOOK SIX

Lyndon B. Johnson

No man of this century, and perhaps no man of any age, ever ascended to the American Presidency with so much raw talent and intuitive skill and so great a preparatory experience in the hard school of politics and public affairs. No man of so much capacity ever had less good fortune in that Presidency.

This is the short, the stirring, the melancholy and the essentially incredible summary of the public life at the summit of power of Lyndon Baines Johnson. He was at once a throwback to a frontier politics redolent of Andrew Jackson and the nineteenth century and the most furiously active innovator of a politics extending in spirit well beyond the twentieth. He was at once the last plainsman in the White House and the first chief executive of an era of space exploration whose arrival he had, more than any other politician, accelerated and welcomed.

In him were met and mingled an old South giving way

to a new; a liberalism in domestic affairs more urgent, more onlooking and more *performing* than ever the country had seen; and a conservatism in foreign policy which would at last help lead to his undoing. His was a second revolution in social legislation far surpassing that of his great mentor, Franklin Roosevelt; his was a mortal collision in foreign affairs between the positions-of-strength philosophy of Roosevelt, Truman, Eisenhower and John Kennedy—and of Johnson himself—and the unacknowledged neoisolationism of an emergent New Left.

Lyndon Johnson, this "Southerner" who was only partly Southern, this first President since Andrew Johnson to have had his whole political roots in the South, had intended his administration to close forever the spiritual and political gap between North and South. He had meant it to replace the Truce of a Hundred Years which had stilled but not liquidated the Civil War with a total if always unspoken treaty of genuine peace and amity. He had meant so to arrange matters that in and after his time there would never again be "a North and a South and an East and a West" but, instead, only one united country where sectionalism was as remote a memory as, say, the Louisiana Purchase.

He had meant, too, to vindicate a century and more of promises and from his day forward to make the American Negro a citizen of the first class in every sense— politically, socially, economically, spiritually—so that racial discrimination would be as unreal and far away in the past in the New America as the events of Fort Sumter and Gettysburg—and Appomattox.

For all this he had in superb measure all the equip-

ment, more professional equipment, indeed, than any
other American President had ever had. His long political career—secretary-ostensible to a Texas Congressman
but Congressman-in-fact even in those distant days, then
himself Member of Congress and then Senator and then
Assistant Democratic Leader of the Senate and then
Democratic Leader and then Vice-President of the
United States—had taught him all that such a career
could possibly teach to one of the most perceptive political minds the nation had produced.

Much that he had intended to reclaim was in fact
reclaimed—nearly all of it, in truth, in the domestic field.
For domestic American liberalism he achieved much
more than any other President of any time. And yet the
more he won for the liberals the more he lost their favor;
and in the end, by towering irony, it was the American
liberals who drove him from office, and it was the American conservatives who felt a sense of elegy and loss in his
departure.

There is among nearly all the Responsibles a recurring
theme of threnody and even of witless tragedy—Truman
disavowed by the wrong people for the wrong reasons;
Taft rejected in the wrong way; Kennedy murdered for
his pains in trying to move civility and tolerance on light
and forbearing feet into the terrain of public affairs. But
to no man and to no time, except perhaps in an incom-
plete and in an inexact sense to Abraham Lincoln and to
his time, has threnody and pointless waste of talented
national leadership been so profound and so real as in the
life and times of Lyndon Johnson.

For the President who in 1964 had won the greatest

popular victory at the polls of record felt compelled in March 1968 to announce his withdrawal from public life —and not in fear that he would not win again but rather in concern that even in winning he would no longer be allowed effectively to govern. It may well be that he could not in fact have won again. For at his left flank, as with Harry Truman before him, the forces of powerful dissidence in his own party had gathered in fierce determination against him. Moreover, though he himself would never in public or private accept this, the vast and at times the overgenerous services he had so long given to domestic liberal causes without for a moment placating liberal opposition had at the same time begun to frighten and to repel that neoconservative and moderate center of opinion which had thus far forgiven his liberal trespasses in deep appreciation for his stout foreign-affairs leadership.

The point, at any rate, is academic. He *did* take himself out of the race. It was in hope that if he wholly removed his personality from the harsh and bitter national debate over the war in Vietnam he might then be able to conclude the war with an acceptable peace free of any suspicion of maneuvering for personal advantage and that he might then be able to serve out his time as at least in part that symbol of the new American Reconstruction which had always been his grand design. And he *did* sincerely question whether even in victory in the election of 1968 his subsequent Presidency could really function, given the venemous infighting that would wrack his own party.

Never had a President who had so lately stood so high

been brought so low—not even Truman, for Truman had at no point stood so high in any case. All that had occurred between the bright mountaintop and the grim and gray valley forms, surely the most amazing, the most dramatic and in some senses the most poignant saga in American politics. No novel, no work of fiction, could possibly offer this story with any hope of credibility—a key word, indeed, in the life and work of Lyndon Johnson.

Many have said that it was the war in Vietnam that "destroyed" Lyndon Johnson. But this is both an understatement and an overstatement. For it was not alone Vietnam, and Johnson's dogged support of the commitment of two previous Presidents to an invaded and a ravaged people, that sent him to the microphone on the night of March 31, 1968, to tell the country that he would neither seek nor accept renomination. Nor is it possible objectively to say that he was wholly destroyed; what would have happened had he decided to run again is wrapped in the enigma of all nonhappenings.

And in any event, no purely rational inquest on what actually occurred, let alone on what might have occurred, is remotely possible. For in his case paradox did not merely occasionally visit the scene; it was howlingly ubiquitous from first to last. Though no President ever tried longer and harder to be popular and liked, it was perfectly plain, and certainly so toward the end, that few Presidents had ever been less successful in that search. In office, he saw more people and more different kinds of people and listened to more points of view than any predecessor had done. Socially, he opened the White

House to more kinds of guests—very often including guests who had dined out on their loud dislike of their host—than any other had done. Personally, he was more forgiving of a sometimes boorish hostility from guests than any other had ever been. Though often and rightly criticized for his tendency to "chew out" staff associates and others in the loudest, the harshest and the most public of ways, he was all the same actually a too-forgiving employer in the vital senses.

He was perfectly capable of hotly raking over a stenographer and then sending her off for two weeks in Bermuda on his money; of dispensing with a staff associate and then presenting him with a $7,000 automobile and a fully gainful future employment personally arranged by Lyndon Baines Johnson. He took an interest in his people—and they were in his mind *his* people. He was capable of strongly criticizing a secretary's hairdo, of sending her at his expense to the most elegant salon in New York, of being worriedly concerned about her health to the point of making personal arrangements for her to go at once to his own physician—at his expense.

He was capable, too, of impulsively picking up the telephone—he always had what is called telephonitis—without the intervention of any buffer-secretary or whatnot, to give to a friend or associate, or at times even to an antagonist, the most thoughtful and sensitive of messages about the greatest or the smallest of matters. He was equally capable of belching at dinner, when he felt like it, and of a curiously old-fashioned courtliness which the public never saw and which, for some arcane reason, he never wanted it to see. He could bellow at the servants, and he could extend to them a genuine kindliness, a wholly unsnobbish friendliness and even an unselfconscious comradeship of one man to another that had to be seen to be credited. It mattered not at all to him the elevated status of some dinner guest of honor; in the mood, he would invite a White House typist, too, and his manner toward the one was no different than toward the other.

He could be at once gravely courteous and loudly rallying toward any guest, toward any friend. The very model of the "new" politics until the much newer New Politics came along, he was nevertheless in some ways deeply traditional and most of all in his attitude toward the Presidency. Faults he had in plenty, but that institution he would never have cheapened had his life depended on it. "Manners" were wholly unimportant to him; *manner* was everything.

Indeed, one of the first of his many and bitter alienations from some of the Washington press corps resulted, in his view, not from press criticism of President Lyndon Johnson but rather from what he considered a breach of manner by guests toward a host who was simply Lyndon Johnson of the LBJ ranch in Texas. Early in his tenure he had gone down to the ranch, accompanied, inevitably, by a press contingent. Feeling the obligations of a host by Texas standards (and there the duty to entertain one's guests is held to be beyond stint), he got into his white convertible and took the correspondents on a literally whirlwind tour of the ranch environs. He had provided beer, though he himself never liked beer and never willingly drank it, preferring not Bourbon, the traditional Southerner's tipple, but Scotch. Thinking to be a good fellow, he himself had a paper cup of beer, meanwhile driving the convertible at eighty miles an hour on the empty roads of Southwest Texas. This was normal driving down there, where one can go twenty miles and never meet another motorist; but the reporters thought it shocking.

Their resulting dispatches made much of the incident, and Johnson on his return to Washington was a study in fury and pained incomprehension. Though he had been many years in politics and though the merest tyro at the game could have told him that, of course, what he did would surely be published, he found it all incredible. "But," he said to a friend, "damn it, these people were my *guests.*" What he saw as a violation of the code of hospitality angered him a great deal more than the substance of the publicity. Just as many of his Presidential actions touched both extremes—in domestic policies a lunge forward into a far tomorrow and in international affairs a dogged support of a traditional past in collective security and containment of Communism—so it often was with the purely personal side of Lyndon Johnson. He was both gregarious and garrulous and highly reticent; now gustily extraverted and again deeply introverted.

On some matters he could be profoundly and even embarrassingly public. There was, for illustration, an occasion in which to assembled reporters he exhibited the scar of a surgical operation and even allowed photographs to be taken. This brought him a spate of contemptuous criticism that, seen in the aftertime, was perhaps

as much responsible as anything else for tireless suggestions in part of the press that he was crude and publicity-
hungry.

Nobody thought to ask him the reason for this performance, and it was this: It was at a time when he had
especially delicate negotiations going on in secret with
European leaders and the White House had been confi-
dentially informed through American intelligence that
rumors of a grave Presidential illness, an illness so critical as to open the possibility of actual disability, were
widely credited in European chancellories. What Johnson was about here was, simply, to be excessively open
in order to still these concerns abroad. He was saying, in
substance, "Yes, I *did* have a serious operation; but that
is the end of it."

Of course the whole affair was most damaging to him
here at home. And he knew it. Yet, he would do nothing
to limit the loss by way of explanation, and beyond
doubt would not have done so even had he been asked the
question. For one of the most deeply lodged of his personal characteristics was an absolute refusal ever to
apologize, on any personal issue, for himself. This was
compounded by an equally immovable conviction that if
a thing was of no real importance, as of course this thing
really was not, "sensible people" should and would
recognize as much. In this regard he was very much like
the ostensibly totally different politician who was Robert Taft. In fact, in the Senate he had held an extraordinary kind of comradeship with Taft. Taft the always
remote and Johnson the sometimes effervescent often
made common human cause there; for both had, in some

things and at some times, a strong and even a belligerent sense of personal privacy.

Again, word once got about that Johnson had the habit of lifting his beagle dog by the ears, and again it was said that proved both a lack of Presidential feeling and an impulse toward cruelty to animals. Johnson was, as always, astonished and uncomprehending, and at length he retorted in an authentically Johnsonian way. On a Sunday afternoon in the spring, while tourists swarmed the environs of the White House, the President collared me and said, "Come on; let's take a walk." He led me, along with the beagle and also a large and handsome dog he called Blanco, down across the Southwest grounds of the White House and straight up to the iron fence against which hundreds of tourists, many of them camera-laden, were pressing. First making certain that their cameras were at the ready, he loudly called the beagle to him and three times lifted it by its ears. The message he was sending across the fence was dual: First (as was indeed the fact) that this sort of treatment did the animal no harm whatever; second that he would pull the beagle's ears when he felt like doing so.

This is another way of saying that he never suffered personal, as distinguished from impersonal, criticism on matters of substance at all gladly. And when it came he would never meet it frontally, feeling that this would dignify attacks he considered merely puerile. This attitude sprang, of course, from a sense of a right to privacy that simply was not attainable in his position, but a right for which he nevertheless stolidly fought until the end. Some put it down to excessive and even bellicose egotism; and, no doubt about it, there was plenty of vanity in this man. For a high sense of one's own value is a part of the make-up of every successful politician; who, without it, could dare even to offer himself for high office?

The difference between Johnson and most other politicians, however, was his inability, his total unwillingness, to mask what (most of the time) he thought of himself. Nor was his prickly defense of his own private actions and habits confined to his own ego. It extended to his friends and associates and especially to those who might have more than the normal quota of human failings and weaknesses. On a Sunday afternoon at the Presidential retreat in Camp David, Maryland, the President was lounging about in the main lodge, called Aspen, with half a dozen old friends and staff members. Most of those present were having a drink or two; the President, as it happened, was not. He was on a diet and, with a stolid lack of cheer, was sipping a soft drink. A latecoming guest to Aspen, a lady with strongly anti-alcohol views, entered at this point, and it was quite evident that she did not like what she saw. Sensing this at once—and his capacity to read other people's attitudes at a glance was sometimes extrasensory—he loudly called out to a mess steward: "Bring me a *double* whiskey!" Why this? The President, though no offender himself, felt that his friends were being criticized unjustly and, worse yet, intrusively.

Again, when the daughter of an old friend had carried collegiate rebellion to the point of suspension and was in much trouble at home, Johnson, bringing along Mrs. Johnson and carrying his first grandchild in his arms, turned up one evening at the friend's home. He deposited the baby on a sofa, beckoned to a Secret Service man carrying covered hampers, and announced, "We've come for dinner, and we've brought it with us." It was at a time when the plate of his Presidency was overfull of seemingly insoluble problems and Johnson himself was reading and hearing on television the most scathing attacks from both his left and his right. He sat for two hours at table without mentioning any public issue but reminiscing, instead, mainly to the daughter of the house, of his own youthful peccadilloes—which he made a good deal more striking than in truth they had been.

At heart he was forever what trial lawyers called "a defense juror," meaning that his sympathies were almost automatically engaged on the side of the one who was being pursued by the many, whether in or out of court. This was why he detested and forbade such techniques as wire-tapping. This was mainly why he was so endlessly patient (some, including this writer, thought too patient altogether) with Negro violence, criticizing it, to be sure, but then adding a rider to the effect that, after all, the Negro had been unfairly treated for two centuries.

Here, he was suspected of being more politically motivated than he was in fact. To the contrary, he knew more than two years before his administration ended that it would be better politics to take a strong law-and-order line. And by this point in time most of the advanced liberals had left him anyhow.

Explainable in the same way was Johnson's concern with schemes to advance the submerged and the underprivileged in every aspect of life. He had known searing poverty as a boy, on a broken-down Texas ranch cursed alike by drought and Depression. He also had been brought up by a Populist father, Sam Johnson, a member of the Texas legislature, to fight and to loathe prejudice, whether racial or religious. Old Sam Johnson, incontestably white Anglo-Saxon Protestant though he was, was one of the first and bravest foes of the modern Ku Klux Klan in Texas, just as his was the strongest voice raised in the legislature against unfairness toward Texans of German background in the hysteria attending the First World War.

Moreover, Sam Johnson was a resolute backer, in good times and in bad, of perhaps the first authentically liberal Governor of Texas, James E. (Pa) Ferguson. And Ferguson, too, though like Lyndon Johnson of old and socially elite Texas stock, broke the mold of his background to become and remain a raffishly compassionate antagonist of that Texas Establishment of which by birth he could have been a charter member.

The long and short of it was that Lyndon Johnson himself grew up with the same sort of motivations and was in all his career persistently opposed by the "rich interests," notably oil, until he became majority leader of the Senate and was too powerful to be further trifled with. It is true enough that later "the interests" accepted him, but it was their surrender and not his. It is true, too, that he became rich himself, but he began with his wife's inherited money and he ended his political life in the not uncommon posture of a very well-heeled politician treating with the rich but genuinely and honestly working most of all for the poor. Though he was always as quick as the next man to turn a penny, or, for that matter a hundred thousand dollars, in a business deal, he really did it all with his left hand and as much in simple gamesmanship as in acquisitiveness. Politics was his obsessive interest, exclusive of everything else, and while he certainly never minded an investment coup, this was very small beer against any political coup.

He was a great politician in some ways and an odd one in other ways. He could and did appeal often to sentiment and occasionally to mere sentimentality. He could and did milk a political situation for its last possible ounce of gain. He could and did seek public favor to an extreme and even self-defeating degree. And yet his worst enemy could not fairly say of him that his political sins ever included the sin of demagoguery. To the contrary, the Johnson who would pick up his beagle by the ears before an audience was a Johnson who fought his very first political campaign—for Congress in Texas— with a belligerent antidemagoguery. He wore the most expensive suits he could find when he could least afford them—and later when he could better afford them. He scorned poor-mouthing of any sort, traveling the backwoods of Texas in the most opulent car he could manage, or even in a then novel helicopter, just as, as Senator, as Vice-President and as President, he presented himself as unapologetically well tailored.

The legend had it that he was forever appealing for popularity, and the legend was partly right. All his life he did have compulsive need to be liked and approved, but it was a subtle and complicated yearning and very far from beseeching, too. What he really wanted, always, was not so much affection for himself personally as acceptance and support for what he wanted to do, and the two motivations were not the same. Had his real drive been only for personal acceptability he would never, he could never, have done many of the things he did. In truth, in strictly personal relationships as a politician he always had a good deal of go-to-hell in his attitude, and he would never knuckle under to the smaller stereotypes of his profession. When he was annoyed he said he was annoyed, and said it very plainly indeed. He would do very much—too much altogether many times—for pressure groups, so long as they did not press him beyond a point. But he could never be pushed by anybody into anything he didn't want to be pushed into in the first place.

And he would *never* (the point is a vital one) use the *personal* protective devices common to most politicians, though he would employ every one in the book for his programs and policies. Though he courted the press, for example, with an assiduity bordering on the obsessive, it was a courtship designed not for Lyndon Johnson as a man but for Lyndon Johnson as a political leader desiring certain things to occur and seeking help in that direction. His personal "public relations" were often ghastly.

In the House, in the Senate, in the Vice-Presidency and in the Presidency he ran his life, both personally and publicly, on the fixed assumption that men and events were alike amenable to and ultimately controlled by sheer rationality. When people acted irrationally or events moved on crazy courses, he was forever amazed and, again like Robert Taft, substantially helpless to cope. Setting out to promise, and ultimately to deliver, to the liberal American political community the widest, the deepest and the most imaginative—and, of course, the most costly—series of domestic reforms in all history, he assumed that his course would be rewarded by liberals and punished by conservatives. This was the rational view; the only trouble with it was that it was also the wrong view.

For the more he did for the liberals in domestic terms the less they liked him for doing it and the more they questioned his motives. The writer Leo Rosten once satirized this extraordinary situation in *Look* magazine. It was, wrote Rosten, as though in his great days with the New York Yankees every home run struck by Joe Dimaggio had been jeered at by the fans because while Dimaggio was, indeed, a strong hitter, he also spoke roughly to the umpire or the bat boy when approaching the plate and anyhow had not really meant to hit the ball as well as he had. Johnson himself would sometimes complain in private that he had outperformed every President in legislative achievement and had been given less credit than any other President. The plaint was objectively a just one; and to identify the reasons for this state of affairs is a hard and subtle task indeed.

It goes without saying that his steadfast refusal to back off from the Vietnam War was a contributing factor, since many of the liberals began violently to attack the policy as the inevitable escalation of the American military commitment became more and more evident. Still, Vietnam was no full explanation; there were many others. For one thing, Johnson's unalterable conviction that pure reason would ultimately sway men caused him to be as heedless in his personal relationships as he was keenly acute in impersonal matters. A good many months after his election in his own right in 1964, a young reporter for the *New York Times* had so urgently appealed for a private interview that he was finally granted it. The President prepared himself for hard questioning on the great issues—Vietnam and so on. His interviewer, however, opened the colloquy with an inquiry about the state of comfort of the White House guards at the gates.

Astonished at this puerility, Johnson burst into incandescent anger and contempt, where a cannier and a more self-protective politician would simply have ignored it. He blazed at his interviewer with very hot language that included four-letter words. The little episode became a big episode. For it was related in Washington and elsewhere as an instance of an excessive Presidential sensitivity to all "criticism," though in fact the only criticism here had been quite the other way around: of Presidential crudity, and of a lack of proper Presidential "style." That it was a most unwise action by the President is, of course, obvious; he should simply have brushed it off. But that it was adequate cause for the furor it raised within the press is debatable. At any rate, this and many other evidences of the President's unhidden distaste for what he believed to be inanity or stupidity played significant parts in the development of a wide public impression that he would brook no criticism and that there was a "credibility gap" about his administration. Highly professional himself, he could scarcely bear amateurism in others—and not at all within the press.

There was just enough truth in the credibility gap legend to cause him great difficulty, but not nearly enough truth in it to warrant the exploitation of it that did his administration such vast harm. To be sure, he *did* have a secrecy complex about some things. Some were merely irritating things, like his frequent and stubborn refusal to tell the reporters when and where he would go and so on. For these there was simply no reason save his reticence about what he considered to be his private affairs. Some instances of his desire for secrecy were highly important and not only justified but quite obligatory. He would not discuss delicate administration plans on matters of high international substance while these plans were in a fluid state. He detested press speculation on such matters, not really for personal reasons but because he supposed, and quite rightly, that premature disclosures of unconcluded negotiations or preparations would harm the national interest and do nobody any real good.

Nevertheless, some correspondents, and especially those who had long believed themselves especially expert in foreign affairs, took the line that he was hiding "the truth" (sometimes in fact when there was *no* "truth," either one way or the other) out of personal hauteur and vainglory. A more patient President, a President more willing to explain himself, might have reduced this form of hostility; Johnson himself after leaving office wrote that his failure in communication here had perhaps been his greatest shortcoming.

Still, the fact of the business is that many members of the press from first to last applied to Johnson criteria they would never have applied to others. To put it plainly, they passed early and easily from criticism to abuse—abuse so violent, indeed, as to bring reproaches from so indisputably objective and detached a working reporter as the dean of the White House correspondents, Merriman Smith of United Press International. Some correspondents, and notably those most emotionally attached to the Kennedy family, began what can only be called an open vendetta against Johnson almost from the day he took office. (Ironically they loved John Kennedy in death far more than they had in life. Ironically, too, some of those who had been far closer to Kennedy—men, for illustration, like columnists Joseph Alsop and Charles Bartlett—behaved with fairness and criticized with responsibility.)

It is not easy for a writer who has spent his adult life as a journalist to write these strictures. But it is necessary as a necessary part of the story of the Presidency of Lyndon Johnson. For this assault was the most savage, the most sustained and the most pitiless of this century, as a good many of the more mature Washington correspondents worriedly recognized, regardless of how they might individually view Johnson as either man or President. The assault came, too, almost exclusively from liberal writers with Democratic party bias and thus had in it the element of journalistic civil war.

The right and the duty to maintain journalistic independence and skepticism, to remain skeptical and critical, was simplified into the privilege and even the obligation to treat the occupant of the White House as an impossibly melodramatic mixture of monster and clown. A frenetic and at times literally hysterical attack upon a man named Johnson became, if unwittingly, an attack upon the integrity and usefulness of the very institution of the Presidency—and this was the infinitely dangerous core of it all. A Justice of the Supreme Court of the United States, a man *a*political by profession and ironically detached in personal character, once told this writer that the atmosphere among the Johnson-haters could in the precisely legal sense be described as senseless and anarchic.

The distinguished Washington *Star* columnist Crosby S. Noyes, a man with neither ideological nor personal attachment to Johnson, described the state of affairs in these words:

Some people may entertain the naïve idea that Presidents dig their own graves, but they don't. When it comes to the projection of a Presidential image to the public the man himself is almost powerless. Whether he has charisma or bad breath, whether he is hero or dolt, is very largely the decision of a few dozen writers, editors and commentators. . . . Lyndon Johnson . . . could pass on to his successor some impressive words of warning about what he may expect. Johnson, so far as the press was concerned, was beaten from the start. History may judge the record of his Administration as among the most significant in this century. Under his leadership the society has advanced further in four years than in the preceding two hundred. In Vietnam, he has done what had to be done in the Nation's highest interests with enormous courage and with complete disregard for his own political future.

Yet, thanks to the press, Johnson, by contemporary judgment, stands repudiated by the American people. Since assuming office at a time of overwhelming national tragedy, he has been the victim of the most savage, implacable and unreasoning attack by powerful segments of the press of any President in American history. The result was the destruction of a great political leader.

The columnist for *Newsweek* magazine, Kenneth Crawford, recalling that Johnson was often condemned in part of the press on such absurdities as his "accent" and his lack of "style," saw, as Noyes had seen, that what was involved here was a great deal more than persistent unfairness to one man in the Presidency. For the "hatchet job," as Crawford called it, that was done on Johnson, mainly by a section of the press so overly devoted to the Kennedy legend as to treat Johnson as a boorish interloper, raised the gravest questions for the future.

Could *any* President emotionally identified by much of the Eastern-based opinion-making media as reflecting some unacceptable geographic and social outland expect not simply rational criticism and resistance but instead a remorseless hostility, right or wrong and willy-nilly? Crawford believed the answer to be at least in doubt as to the Johnson successor, Richard Nixon. So did Noyes. So did other responsible political writers. And so did this writer. In any event the burden of proof is, on any objective analysis, overwhelming that Johnson suffered precisely such an unthinking hostility from what in

Washington was commonly called a "Kennedy press" whose operations were so utterly removed from the spirit of the man for which it was named, John F. Kennedy himself.

That there *was* such a press and that it was deeply unfair has been testified to by a man who was, as he himself says, a part of it all, Stewart Alsop. Writing in the near afterlight of the 1968 Democratic National Convention that chose Hubert H. Humphrey as its nominee after Johnson's retirement, Alsop observed that it seemed then "a good time to try to be fair to Lyndon Johnson." He went on, "That is never easy, because he has so often been unfair to other people. But a lot of people (especially journalistic admirers of President Kennedy, including this one) have been brutally unfair to him."

This confession again establishes the point that what was involved here was a great deal more than journalistic injustice to a man called Lyndon Johnson. For Alsop correctly wrote this epilogue:

Lyndon Johnson could almost certainly have bulled his way through to renomination and quite possibly to reelection. To abandon power goes against the man's every instinct; yet he chose to do so. He so chose for several reasons, some not unconnected with his colossal pride. But the main reason, surely, was simple love of country.

He knew the country would have to pay a terrible price, in what he called in his March 31 speech "divisiveness," if he ran again. He chose not to make the country pay that price. For that—as well as for much else for which he received little credit—Lyndon Johnson deserves the heartfelt thanks of his countrymen.

The long and short of it is that in Johnson's time the traditional forms of criticism and contention in politics were widely abandoned by his intramural antagonists in press and politics alike. It ended in a bloodless assassination of Johnson himself by men who scorned and fought him for what rationally should have been in their eyes the best of his qualities and for reasons so grotesquely illogical as literally to force to his defense other men who in another climate would have been in the forefront of his critics. Though he had mortally offended the South on the civil rights and antipoverty issues and though nearly the whole of his domestic program was in the deepest sense unacceptable to conservative philosophy, the point was reached where his basic support came most of all from moderate Southerners and conservative Republicans.

These two groups did not, of course, abandon resistance to his domestic policies; they did, however, feel compelled to mute their voices on these matters for more reasons than respect for his posture in Vietnam. They were motivated quite as much by awareness that "dissent" in this country was being carried into mania by the most fundamentally shocking emotional disarray within the Democratic party in political history. Where he himself ultimately feared that even a renewed Presidential mandate would not for a moment be accepted by his in-party opposition, the whole body of sentient conservatives feared for the very future of responsibility in politics and for the life of the two-party system. They were appalled, moreover, by what was scarcely less than a new and frightening and precious sectionalism in politics more dangerous to orderly government, because more subtle and harder to get at, than the old simplistic divisions over the Mason-Dixon Line which Johnson himself had sought so hard to heal.

So it came about that the greatest allies of the Johnson Presidency in its later years were found among men who detested his domestic innovations—Dwight Eisenhower prominently among these—but who recoiled far more from what they believed to be the evolution of a politics of total irresponsibility. They saw in the adult political scene something roughly equivalent to the postadolescent campus marches and protests and demonstrations, which now became not instances of free speech by any definition but rather of violent assaults upon duly constituted authority in all its forms and upon the constitutional conduct of foreign policy itself.

Eisenhower called quietly and often upon Johnson in those days, withholding none of his concerned opposition to Johnson's domestic course but nevertheless supporting him as *President* for larger reasons. Harry Truman was in much the same mood—and so, one is morally convinced, would John Kennedy have been had he been alive. Senator Everett McKinley Dirksen of Illinois, the Republican leader of the Senate, wryly took up the strangely ambivalent course forced upon him by a world that none of the Responsibles had ever made. He fought Johnson domestically; he backed Johnson in foreign policy; and most of all he backed Johnson's right to *be*

President. So did many another Republican partisan; so, very quietly, did many a Southern Senator, notwithstanding that the name "Johnson" had become a bad word in their homeland.

The President's attitude toward all this was a nearly indescribable blend of gratitude, embarrassment and chagrin. One night he told a dinner guest of an Eisenhower visit of that afternoon, saying, "God, how that man has helped me!" He reflected a moment and then went on: "I don't know what I would do without his help in foreign policy."

The guest asked, "What did he say about your Great Society?"

There was a pause and then Johnson smiled. "Don't ask about *that.*"

Thus it was that the President who had so keenly pursued the concept of a national consensus as to open himself to accusations that he wanted to be everything to everybody found his sole ultimate consensus of support to be formed most of all of his traditional opposition. Even more striking was that this whole state of affairs, the whole irrational nature of the thing, foreclosed any possibility of an adult national dialogue upon the true substance of the Johnson administration, upon its logical merits and demerits.

There was debate aplenty about the Vietnam War and about foreign and military policy in general, but this was roughly as arid as debate in Truman's time had been over the fall of mainland China and, for that matter, over the Korean War. For with some distinguished exceptions—one thinks here of such Senators as John Sherman

Cooper of Kentucky and George Aiken of Vermont—
the anti–Vietnam War politicians directed their case
more at the person of Lyndon Johnson than at what he
was doing and not doing. Too, in exercising the longest
and most vehement and most publicized "dissent" in
history they filled the national air with cries that dissent
was being stifled. But identifiable and understandable
alternatives to the policy in Vietnam were notably lacking in the rhetoric of such as Senator J. William Fulbright of Arkansas, the chairman of the Senate Foreign
Relations Committee, and Senator Mike Mansfield of
Montana, both of whom were tirelessly seeking the head
of the head of their party in the White House.

It was impossible for many onlookers—and for President Johnson—not to suppose on all the evidence that
what the more extreme "doves" really wanted, but
would never say, was simply an American withdrawal
from South Vietnam and thus the abandonment of the
commitments of Eisenhower, Kennedy and Johnson. To
be sure, other critics, such as the late Senator Robert F.
Kennedy of New York, *did* propose actions short of actual surrender, but all such proposals were much easier
to utter than to implement in any responsible way.

The net of it all was that the main thrust of the doves
was simply for getting out of Vietnam at any cost, and
for leaving both rationale and rationalization for later.
Johnson therefore found himself caught up in a situation
in which the most articulate of his nominal leaders in the
Senate were not only mortally opposed to his whole
stance in Vietnam but were persistently unclear as to
their own prescription for altering that stance. The right

wing had pitilessly condemned Truman for the fall of China, without ever showing how they themselves would or could have saved China. So Johnson became a victim for not replacing a policy in Vietnam with the best that the left wing could offer—which was either a nonpolicy or a policy of cut-and-run carried out under other words.

What the left wing was really bemoaning, as the right wing had done in Truman's time, was the reality of world affairs. Moreover, again as in Truman's time, Johnson's adversaries had to find a devil to beat. And they found him. The wheel had turned all the way around. The conspiracy theory of politics which had been applied in the Truman years now became, against Johnson, the theory that an essentially brutal, certainly vain, surely unlettered and obviously graceless cowboy-President was hanging on in Vietnam simply out of crass and monumental obstinacy. The more he offered concessions—and sometimes excessive concessions, if measured realistically—to the invading North Vietnamese Communists and the indigenous Vietcong, the more it was said of him that only his lack of "flexibility" stood in the way of peace.

Increasingly obsessed with a logically weak case and increasingly bound by their own emotional investment to prove Johnson's wrongness, the more excited doves, in politics and in the press, turned upon him the longest and at its worst the most punishing character-lashing ever known in this country. In the preparation of this book I commissioned a professional researcher to study

President-baiting in its more extreme forms. Literally exact findings or analogies in such matters are, of course, impossible to make. With this qualification, however, the conclusion was that while every President beginning with Washington had been called many hard names and while such "strong" ones as Lincoln and Franklin Roosevelt had known much calumny, no President had ever been so limitlessly and so venomously attacked *ad hominem and within his own party*. The word "murderer" was not often applied to Johnson by a public figure, but synonyms for murderer were commonplace, and sometimes from the floor of the Senate.

Now the enduring pity here was that, as again was the case on domestic issues, the Vietnam debate early degenerated into mostly shrill name-calling by the opposition, and never had in the first place the vital element of straightforwardness from the advanced dove side. The old isolationists of the thirties may have been very wrong—and were in my opinion profoundly so—but it must be said of them that they never dissimulated. They wanted this nation to remain aloof from "Europe's wars," and to their credit they said as much in so many words. The Vietnam issue, to the contrary, saw the birth of a new isolationism, strongly touched with simple, old-fashioned pacifism, that was never acknowledged; and with this Johnson simply could never come effectively to grips. A perfectly arguable case could have been made that we should never have gone into Vietnam in the first place and thus should get out totally and forthwith, confessing, if necessary, an earlier national error, and letting it go at that. No such case, however, was ever made or even seriously attempted.

At all events, Johnson's removal of himself, as a personal object of abrasiveness, from the Presidential struggle never remotely achieved its aim of calming the national atmosphere and of withdrawing the poison from public controversy. It all went on quite as bitterly after he had left the race as when he had presumably been in it; nor did his unexampled personal sacrifice in the matter for a moment placate his adversaries. This circumstance is vital to any understanding of the strange case —indeed, the tragic case, as Eric Goldman has denominated it—of Lyndon Johnson.

For what it suggests is that in Lyndon Johnson's era the country experienced, but did not and could not generally recognize, a syndrome of essentially glandular dislike of a President which had no real precedent and simply could not be approached in the ordinary terms of rational inquiry. The effect was Mad Hatterism. On the one hand he was vilified almost beyond belief. On the other hand the genuine and major shortcomings of his administration were substantially ignored to the point where there was, from first to last, almost no substantial critical analysis of the revolutionary course in social matters to which he was committing his nation or of such issues as an unexampled rise in crime and public disorder and an equally unexampled rise of permissiveness across the whole of society.

Viewed without passion, his administration saw the highest profits, the highest wages, the lowest real unemployment and the widest diffusion of the supposedly good things of material life and at the same time the most febrile and vaguely angry and disenchanted public mood in the nation's experience. It saw the greatest of all advances in civil rights, accompanied step by step by the most sullen of moods among the leaders of the minorities. It did more for all forms of education at all levels, notably and uniquely so at the college level, and it saw also the shrillest and most pervasive campus hatred of a President. It did more for disadvantaged children, for the old and the sick, for the blind and the disabled, than had been done by government in all the nearly two centuries that had gone before. It did not neglect the rich and the comfortable, either. And yet . . . and yet. The principal author of all these things, whose mastery of Congress was, even with its lapses, the most productive ever seen, was so unacceptable to a highly articulate few as to leave office openly scorned by a self-denominated elite and ill regarded by the many.

So palpably was this true that Johnson had tears in his eyes when, just before his departure from Washington after the induction of the Nixon administration, a plainly affectionate crowd of ordinary people gathered about the home of Clark Clifford, the President's last Secretary of Defense, to peer through the windows at a farewell party that was taking place there and to raise hand-painted signs saying, "They'll miss you, LBJ." Johnson would not trust himself to respond; he turned brusquely away from the windows and walked upstairs in the Clifford house, there to remain until it was time for him to go to the airport for the trip home to Texas.

In his last days in office he had occupied himself with giving to Richard Nixon the most helpful of briefings and, by Nixon's own estimate, the most generous support ever seen in a time of Presidential transition from one party to the other. The end, indeed, like the beginning, was undeniably successful, whatever might have been said about all that had gone on in between. The fact was that Johnson was at his best in moments of the very highest drama and crisis and at his worst when the times and circumstances called only for slogging through. Bigness was both his highest attribute and, carried, as sometimes it was, too far and too heedlessly, his greatest practical fault. The quality led him into an imperious attitude at times and also into an excessive tolerance of dangerous disloyalties among associates and of cross-purpose disarray among subordinate policy makers. When he was impatient he was too impatient altogether, a kind of "El Supremo," as one of his staff people once called him in exasperated affection.

And when he was patient, he was too patient altogether. When he entered the Presidency in November 1963, by the accident of the assassination in Dallas, he confronted in that instant one crisis that was soluble and one crisis that was to turn out to be insoluble, whatever his skill and whatever his effort. The first was, of course, the crisis of confidence in a nation gripped in the shock and horror of its leader's assassination. Here was a supreme test of the capacity of the political system to sustain effective national unity, not to say national health and even national order, in the wake of the most frightful wounds to national spirit and to national morale since Lincoln was shot. This supreme trial Johnson met and mastered with a sensibility and a common-sensibility never matched in any similar national convulsion.

In literally blood-spattered surroundings he took the

oath of the Presidency in a parked aircraft in Dallas bearing the body of his slain predecessor, not knowing whether his old friend and protégé, Governor John Connally of Texas, who had himself been shot by the assassin, was now alive or dead. Johnson, who had long been a "socialist" or even a "Communist" to his right-wing adversaries in Texas and a Tory Bourbon to his left-wing critics in the North and East, now assumed in the worst possible circumstances the burden of preventing chaos in his country from one political extreme or the other. The flight back to Washington bore both the body of the fallen President and his unutterably troubled successor; and Johnson for the first time in his political life was moved to do what this sometimes strangely reserved politician had never done—publicly to call upon God for help.

It was a journey of high tragedy marred by some incidents that hardly bore repeating—incidents of sick and unreasoning animus toward the new President by some but certainly not all of the stricken aides of the old President—and it was, all in all, a nightmare unexampled in the life of this republic. Johnson himself, recognizing that now the whole onus for the country's safety and sanity lay upon him, also preoccupied himself and indeed all but tortured himself, then and later, to lift, if by the smallest of touches, the grief that lay upon Mrs. Kennedy, upon the Kennedy people generally and, of course, upon the country itself.

He returned to Washington to the private house that had been his home as Vice-President and for critical days thereafter operated not from the White House, with its matchless communications, but rather in suburban surroundings never meant for the discharge of any heavy responsibility. Sometimes he used the telephone himself at The Elms, the house he had purchased as Vice-President. Always, however, in the initial period of maximum crisis, he remained awake day and night tirelessly gathering up the reins of government; reassuring the dead President's Cabinet officers that they would be his own Cabinet officers; making a score of critical decisions with subordinates with whom his sole communication was sometimes only over the telephone. The White House was reserved in this period for the Kennedy family; this was at Johnson's order and he never complained of the consequences.

Among these decisions so informally reached in a suburban household—if a rich and elegant one—was one in effect to remove the murder of John Kennedy from the moral jurisdiction of the authorities of Texas by the appointment of the high commission which, under Chief Justice Earl Warren, would investigate the assassination. This was no easy thing to do, for Texas was, after all, Johnson's own state, and what he was in substance saying here was that the officials of that state could not be trusted in this matter. The President here accepted the recommendation of his old friend Abe Fortas, later a Johnson appointee to the Supreme Court, though it may in fact have been in Mr. Johnson's mind in any case. At all events, this was an unprecedented change in effective jurisdiction, and it never would have been ordered had the assassination occurred anywhere but in Texas.

Next was Johnson's decision to keep all the old

Kennedy associates, Cabinet and otherwise, as long as he
could and as trustingly as he could. This meant that he
was forgoing the indispensable prerogative of a President to be surrounded only by his own choices. And
while it was an act of self-abnegation in one sense, it was
clearly necessary in another. For to have dispensed with
any of the Kennedy people at this emotional juncture
could have been seen as crude and insensitive. The trouble was, however, that once having adopted the policy
Johnson followed it both too far and too long. In the
White House he had assistants who had openly scorned
and demeaned him in his days as Vice-President; a favorite amusement of some of the Kennedy people in those
days had been to throw darts at a mounted photograph
of "Old Cornpone"—Lyndon Johnson. In the White
House, too, he had assistants who were secretly meeting
within a week of Kennedy's death to prepare a method
to discredit the new President and thus to deny him
renomination in 1964, in favor of Robert F. Kennedy.
And in the Cabinet, he long had one official, Robert
Kennedy, the Attorney General, whose hostility was total and implacable. In the Cabinet, too, he had others
who in all Johnson's Presidency served him only in the
formal sense and reserved their whole emotional attachment for Robert Kennedy or for his brother, Senator
Edward Kennedy.

To an onlooker who happened to have an intimate
view of the scene it seems quite fair to say in retrospect
that for most of his five years in the White House Lyndon Johnson had precisely two Cabinet associates who
unreservedly supported him, in good times and bad, and

who were *unqualifiedly* loyal to him personally—Secretary of State Dean Rusk and Secretary of the Treasury Henry H. Fowler.

As to the White House staff itself, nearly all the old Kennedy people gradually left; some in honorable disaffection, like Theodore Sorensen and Kenneth O'Donnell and Arthur Schlesinger, Jr., and Pierre Salinger, and some with protestations of undying affection that turned very shortly into an excess of animus toward LBJ. Again, the press secretary who served Johnson longest, Billy Don Moyers, somehow gained kudos from Johnson critics, again mainly the Kennedyites, in almost exact ratio to the denunciations heaped upon Johnson in the press with which Moyers was working.

All in all, in a word, the President's situation as to advisers was inherently an impossible one. It would have been soluble in the end only by stolidly judicious dismissals such as Harry Truman had handed to the disloyal Henry Wallace and James Byrnes—but this time the pink slips never arrived. Johnson's motivations in all this were enigmatically opaque and mixed in both political and human terms. His first notion, to keep civilized communication open to the Kennedy faction to the last possible moment, had been perfectly sound. A time came, however, and especially after he had so overwhelmingly won the Presidency in his own right from Barry Goldwater in 1964, when it was plain that in his own household sat his most implacable and his most dangerous antagonists. And still he did not move, and he never did, right to the end.

Why? Beyond doubt, he was deeply and lastingly

grieved by the murder of John Kennedy and had, and
retained, a genuine desire to deal softly with any and all
of Kennedy's political heirs. Johnson was always a man
of ready sentiment, and he was also a man of the most
dogged obstinacy. A part of the explanation here surely
lies in his determination that, damn it all, he *would* at last
bring over his enemies. A part lies in his high resistance
to unsolicited advice, and especially from those conservative sources who were inevitably most prone here to
urge him to "get tough." Too, the interpretation common at the time that what was going on was a "Johnson-
Kennedy feud" was in his eyes nonsense. He had known
Robert Kennedy as a boy in staff work around the Senate
when Lyndon Johnson was a Senate grandee. One lobe
of the Johnson political brain recognized that Kennedy,
boy or not, was becoming a genuine threat, but the patriarchial Johnson lobe simply could not really see it this
way. To Johnson it was no "feud"; this term overstated
the case a great deal. He never gladly bore Kennedy's
hostility and intraparty attacks, but his attitude, even in
private, could have been described as more a weary anger, mixed with exasperated incomprehension, than hatred or malice. The point was that Johnson-the-rational
persistently believed that Kennedy's attitude was essentially self-defeating, if only because it clearly created
envenomed divisions within the Democratic party, and
that in time Kennedy himself must surely recognize as
much.

As to staff members, the President kept every one,
however difficult, however disloyal for that matter, with
a kind of absent-minded tolerance which had also a good

deal of "why bother?" within it. The truth is that he was at heart a nonstaff, nonorganization kind of politician, far from enchanted with tables of organization and personnel graphs and any and all committee or group exercises. The truth, that is to say, is that down underneath he thought he could do it all himself, if it came to that, and very nearly he could and did. Nor did he believe very much in the staff-specialist theory, save for the important exception of foreign policy. He had a houseful of Special Assistants, each fitted out with a sort of elegant diploma on the wall proclaiming that in this fellow the President reposed special trust and confidence. In reality the only real specialist in the Johnson White House was Walt W. Rostow, his foreign-policy adviser. All the others were expected to take up an oar in any boat that had to be rowed along, sometimes hotly chivvied along by the President himself, sometimes paid the highest and the most generous of Presidential compliments.

Indeed, when a major Johnson speech was in preparation the President's basic trust in the generalist was illustrated amply. Half a dozen men might be simultaneously working on this utterance, with Johnson himself sitting at the far end of a telephone giving instructions, advice, admonitions and thanks first to one and then to another. He had an extravagant respect for writers simply as such, as ironically he had for all able to call themselves intellectuals, and his general notion was that the more writers the better. And yet when a speech was at last done, it turned out to be about eighty per cent Johnson and twenty per cent the other four or five or six laborers

253

in prose. Somehow, at the end of it all he impressed his own final ideas and also his own rhetoric on the ostensible product of the many. Too, some of his best-remembered passages were thrown in strictly ad lib but never appeared to have been; his Senate training had taught him how to interpolate in a prepared address without breaking stride.

And yet, for all the multiplicity of assistants, advisers, consultants, writers and "idea men" who surrounded him, the ultimate truth was that for five years Lyndon Johnson was, in all his moments of truth, even more poignantly alone than any other modern occupant of the White House had been except Kennedy. Nearly all politicians tend to make more strenuous effort to bring in converts than to defer to the followers they have already got; this is a simple necessity of their art. With Johnson, however, as in so many other things, the truism was carried beyond known example. The more his least loyal associates showed in the plainest of human ways their lack of affection for him—but, oddly, rarely any lack of respect for him, however grudgingly granted—the more he worked in compulsive determination to *make* them like him.

And, as it happened, the more recalcitrant were all advanced liberals; and it was precisely to these, and never to his undemanding conservative friends and supporters, that the President turned an unfailingly placatory face. That it did him no good any more than his unsurpassed legislative achievements in behalf of domestic liberalism ever did him any good never for a moment altered his determination to go on with the same line.

Continuously described during his Presidency as exceptionally hard to get along with, the improbable truth was that so far as his staff and Cabinet were concerned his shortcoming was the precise reverse: he never required others to get along with him.

His faith in the efficacy of persuasion (which he so often indicated by the use of the spiritual admonition "come, let us reason together") became a dogma so entrenched within him that he would never and could never accept the all-too-plain reality that in his circumstances persuasion simply was never going to be effective. He literally pursued the dissident and the disrespectful, not because in any substantive sense he really had to have them but because something in him would never allow him to concede, even to himself, that his approach was manifestly not succeeding. Nor is this somewhat complicated psychological explanation the only explanation.

In all his career Johnson had a lively appreciation of offbeat men, of what in colloquialism would be called ornery men, just as he never had much respect for conventional men or "organization men." He liked to forgather, both professionally and socially, with the politically irreverent and the personally "difficult" types, and he had very little time for those whose thoughts and habits were highly predictable. He preferred to hone his own notions and attitudes against the sharp and the acid rather than the bland and easy.

Confronted with a conformist bore, whether a politician or a guest, he was himself openly bored—and his manner could be just short of outrageous. When, in 1960, for illustration, a naïve young foreign diplomat asked the then Senate majority leader at a dinner party whether he was *really* running for the Presidency, Johnson replied with a courtesy so extreme as to become parody, "Oh, good heavens, no! My highest ambition would be to see Dick Russell (Senator Richard Brevard Russell of Georgia) become President—in the hope that perhaps he would allow me to become his appointments secretary!"

Once, the late Daisy Harriman, a splendid old dowager queen of the Democratic party, had been picking at Majority Leader Johnson to ask approval by the Senate of a bill looking toward some form of self-rule in the District of Columbia. This matter had, understandably, not been at the top of his priorities; but at length he had bowed to Daisy's will and put the bill through, though softened a bit to permit its passage. Mrs. Harriman, no lady to abandon any of her prickly independence in any circumstances, gave him at a dinner party what was far less a vote of thanks for his efforts than a sturdy complaint that he had not done much more while he was about it.

Other guests were slightly embarrassed, expecting a Johnsonian explosion. To the contrary, he beamed fondly upon Mrs. Harriman and then bode his time. Shortly the opportunity came for the kind of retort, a toughish reply to a toughish thrust, that greatly amused him. When Mrs. Harriman asked him what Senator was on the whole most helpful to him in bearing his responsibilities as the Democratic leader of the Senate, supposing, of course, that he would respond with some good Democratic name, he replied, "Why, Daisy, George Malone, of course." Malone was a right-wing Republican Senator who was both anathema to Daisy Harriman and a great nuisance to the entire Democratic party.

Still, to capture the uncapturable was not alone Johnson's motive in his long and unavailing search among his critics. An even stronger—and an even stranger—one lay in the circumstance that, again all through his career, he was invariably far more disturbed by liberal than by conservative criticism and far more automatically anxious to answer and to disperse the one than the other. He could easily toss off conservative attacks; liberal attacks burned deeply within him, no matter the occasion, no matter the office he held. In the Senate years no less than in the Presidency, except, of course, less visibly so, he seemed somehow to feel personally at fault when liberal colleagues criticized him; when the conservatives did so, he simply smiled and changed the subject.

Because he had reached the Senate majority leadership with heavy and critical Southern sponsorship, most notably that of Senator Russell of Georgia, it was widely supposed that he was essentially a Southern agent there. No estimate could have been more wrong. For Johnson was always in but never of the Southern world of the Senate. He had the right personal background and the right geography, but very much the wrong ideas. The first circumstance inevitably earned him the forgiveness of the Southerners in times of intraparty crisis; at such times they spoke of him with the pained and exasperated affection of some Back Bay Bostonian uncle toward a nephew who had, through the mystery of providence, chosen to transport himself to San Francisco there to become a hippie in the Haight-Ashbury. After all, Lyndon's grandfather had been a Confederate soldier, and, well . . .To see the attitude of such an Old South patriarch as the late Senator Harry Flood Byrd, Sr., to "Lyndon" when Lyndon, as not infrequently, was coaxing his Southern brethren into the most wildly improbable legislation from their viewpoint was to see real-life theater. The Southerners appreciated his virtuosity even while they deplored its consequences—and these consequences were to run a good deal further than they had ever supposed.

For one of the indestructible legends left from Johnson's Senate years, years which by all but common consent marked him down as perhaps the ablest majority leader of all time, was the legend of the "operator," of the "arm-twister," of the politician insufficiently sensitive to means in the pursuit of ends. As in nearly all folklore, there was some truth in this; as in much of folklore, there was also a great deal of towering nonsense.

It is true that Johnson was a master of oneupmanship, of gamesmanship, long before those traits entered the language. It is true that in the Senate (and in the Presidency, too) he tirelessly worked every lever of power, large or small, to forward his designs. It is true that in this process he used cajolery, flattery and humor, pleasant and mordant; that he returned favor for favor; that those who stood against him had no difficulty in sensing that he did not at all like what they were doing. What is quite untrue, however, makes an equally formidable list. It is untrue that he was never concerned by means; it is untrue that he used threats or any other form of blackmail; it is untrue that he carried grudges; it is untrue that he "paid back" those who voted against him. It is also untrue that to him the game itself was more important than the objectives of the game, but the error in comprehension here was a pardonable one.

For precisely because he was a born politician, in the sense that Isaac Stern, say, might be said to be a born violinist, he *did* openly and gustily enjoy political maneuver in all its forms. Give him a political problem to surmount or to finesse and this was happiness to Lyndon Johnson. Thus it was that very often, in whatever office he occupied, he would tell friends or callers or interviewers in the greatest of detail of his coups and triumphs. It was all, in that sense, a big chessboard to him and he delighted in every move upon it. What he never did, however, was solemnly to explain to friend or caller or interviewer that his thrusts and turns upon this chessboard were in aid of much bigger, and often much finer, things. The omission was enormously important and enormously harmful to him. And yet, given his character and personality, both of which were intractable, he *could not* have so explained himself.

To say aloud when he had passed the first substantial civil rights bill since Reconstruction, as in fact he had done in 1957, that he was doing this in order to grant justice at last to an abused minority, would have been in the most literal sense impossible to him—a good deal like praying aloud in Church. He always assumed that certain things could be left unsaid and would be assumed by others; he always recoiled, too, from overt "niceness" or evangelical postures. (This latter circumstance, parenthetically, went also to his religious feeling. Formal church practices made him vaguely uneasy; but very informal church practices, though in his personal tradition, were not to his personal taste.)

At any rate, the unexampled leadership successes in the Senate turned into far more of a curse than a boon. Millions of Americans came to believe that he was perhaps not "sincere"; others saw him as a kind of darkly competent but uncaring President. It became politically possible, for example, to accuse him of lack of feeling for the death and horror of Vietnam—this of the man I saw weep in private, on many an occasion, when an aide brought him in the nighttime a top-secret signal of the day's casualties in Vietnam. Because he was so widely pictured as "tough," as indeed in some ways and at some times he was, it became fashionable to see him as also uncaring.

And again there occurred a massive collision between fact and legend in which legend triumphed and fact was lost. For the Johnson so often pictured as a hardhanded war-lord sort of President was in truth a Johnson whose political homeland was basically that of populism; and populism is far more attached, generally, to pacifism than to militarism. The truth was that Lyndon Johnson's whole Congressional experience had been far more that of a skeptical gadfly to the military than a disciple of "The Brass." His own brief military service as a naval officer in the Second World War, from which he emerged with a Silver Star, had left him at heart much more anti-Pentagon than pro-Pentagon. Moreover, the man who until very nearly the end was his Secretary of

Defense, Robert S. McNamara, was so emotionally anti-Brass as to excite valid concern among senior officers.

The extraordinary reality, in brief, was that when Johnson said over and over that no man in the United States could more prayerfully yearn for peace than himself, he spoke the truth. Attacks upon him by the anti–Vietnam War Democratic Left actually evoked in him more grief than anger—though anger, too, there was in plenty. His whole drive as a politician was to do things for people and not to them; schemes for human betterment did not simply occupy him; they preoccupied him to a point little short of obsession.

And yet, central to his whole understanding of the Presidency was the conviction that vital national interests abroad and national honor—he did not shy from this old-fashioned expression, whatever its undertones of Colonel Blimpism and "imperialism" to his violently hostile Left—stood at the very top of Presidential obligations. Thus, while he was often and sometimes rightly said to be too concerned with what the public opinion polls might be reading, he stood one night in the family quarters of the White House and said to a friend, "The polls are going down and down and down, and the chicken-hearted, even among my friends, are leaving me, too. But I'll tell you this: If my goddamn poll sinks to minus eight per cent I'm going on out there [in Vietnam]. Sometimes a President has got to be *President.*"

Was he, then, noble in fortitude, wrong or right though his policy might seem? In the sense that knowingly and deliberately he allowed the dissolution of his administration for his policy, the answer is yes. In the sense that he only did what in the most profound human definition he *had* to do, the answer is no. For in this capacity he was what any honorable commander is in action: he saw his duty plain and he did it. That he made mistakes here, quite apart from the central question of the wisdom or unwisdom of his actions, is incontestable.

Somehow he was never able fully to explain all of Vietnam to all of the country. But while this was a large shortcoming, he was never small in meeting it. From beginning to end he allowed no subordinate to accept any kind of blame for Vietnam; from beginning to end he never forgot those, headed by the memorably courageous Dean Rusk, who never faltered at his side. However staggering with fatigue, however lashed and beaten by his adversaries, Johnson never omitted in any gathering with Rusk and the others to rally their spirits, often with a wry self-deprecation that was far from common to this proud and self-willed man, or to tell them plainly to leave the worrying at last to him.

So much was this the case, for illustration, that he nominated himself to be the final judge as to where and how the controversial American bombing operations in North Vietnam would be conducted. The anti-military-minded denounced him for this, saying that it only proved anew his thirst for blood and violence. Johnson himself explained it to a friend in rather different terms. "Bob McNamara is carrying a fearful load already. Damned if I'm going to put this load onto him, too. If *he* is identified as the decision maker, they will beat hell out of him every time a bomb falls wrong. But they will beat hell out of me anyhow, so what's the difference? I *need* that fellow; I want to keep him just as long as I can."

McNamara departed before the whole road had been run, to be succeeded by Clark Clifford. Still, as the long ordeal of the principal "hawk" at the White House and of the other hawks around him ran on to its bitter end, not all was melancholy amidst the surrounding gloom. For while taken as a whole the "Johnson team" was never very much of a team for him, the real team drew strength, much as a battered infantry division will draw it, from the very grandeur, if a somber grandeur, of its obligations. Rusk, Fowler, Walt Rostow—these hardy characters never wavered or flinched—never "shimmied when the knife is at the belly," as the President put it— nor did *he*.

Repeatedly he sought to appease the most savage of his intraparty adversaries—men like Senators J. William Fulbright of Arkansas and Robert Kennedy of Massachusetts—and here, too, the famous "feuds" of the time were far more on their side than on his. The official Democratic leader of the Senate, Mike Mansfield of Montana, was, next to Fulbright and Kennedy, perhaps the most unappeasable and most troublesome of the Senate "doves." Not far behind was Senator Eugene McCarthy, the man who first challenged the President from within his own party by way of the Presidential primary.

And, for another of the endless list of ironies that gathered about Johnson, three of these four had been recipients of special Johnsonian favors in the past. Fulbright became chairman of the Foreign Relations Committee only through Johnson's adroit act of persuasion in causing the aged Senator Theodore Francis Green of Rhode Island to give up that post. Mansfield was personally placed by Johnson upon the leadership ladder in the Senate; by Johnson's appointment he became majority whip; by Johnson's subsequent recommendations as Vice-President to President Kennedy, Mansfield was confirmed as floor leader. Solely through Johnson's "wheeling and dealing" Senator McCarthy was put onto the powerful and prestigious Finance Committee the week he reached the Senate. No Senator ever before had arrived on that committee without long prior dog's-body service.

Johnson, moreover, had seriously considered McCarthy for his Vice-President running mate in 1964, before finally settling upon the Senator's colleague from Minnesota, Hubert H. Humphrey. Thus when, less than four years later, Eugene McCarthy took the extraordinary step of openly contesting Johnson's renomination by entering the nation's earliest primary, that of New Hampshire in March 1968, with ceaseless attacks upon the Vietnam War, it was to the harassed man in the White House a pretty howdy-do indeed. He had always "liked Gene"; and even now that "Gene" was seeking his vitals Johnson's private attitude was not so hostile as might have been supposed. He had a certain bleak appreciation of the circumstances that, political enemy or not, "Gene" was at least an honest foeman; and of course there was also the element of undoubted courage in what McCarthy was attempting.

Senator McCarthy, in fact, ran a strong second in New Hampshire, though Johnson himself was represented only by proxy there. And while the President suffered no outright repudiation in New Hampshire, as another President, Harry Truman, had suffered it there in 1952, at the hands of Senator Estes Kefauver of Tennessee, the returns made very poor reading at the White House. Some of the more enthusiastic McCarthy backers, in truth, took the line then and maintained it later that Senator McCarthy had "forced" Johnson to retire from the race. This actually was carrying the thing much too far. No substantial body of informed opinion doubted that Johnson could have had the nomination in any event, McCarthy or no McCarthy, even if a second and later-coming adversary, Senator Robert F. Kennedy, had not been brutally assassinated in Los Angeles. A far weaker candidate offered in his stead by Johnson, Vice-President Hubert H. Humphrey, easily defeated the McCarthy challenge at the subsequent Democratic National Convention in Chicago—a convention stained by unprecedented anti-Johnson and anti-Humphrey rioting from left-wing student organizations and by a sometimes brutal counterviolence from Mayor Richard Daley's police force.

The whole business—New Hampshire and then the horror of Chicago—on superficial reading identified Eugene McCarthy as the President's enemy. But he never himself took quite that view of the matter, of which he was actually able to take a fairly objective view since more than a year before that infinitely bitter month of March he had determined not to run again and had so told me, in strict confidence, in the presence of Mrs.

Johnson, at the Presidential retreat in Maryland, Camp David.

No, to Johnson McCarthy was never quite the destructive force as was, say, Senator Fulbright of the Foreign Relations Committee. Fulbright's position made him far the more influential in the one area where, in the end, Johnson thought that the maximum harm had been done to his foreign-policy leadership—that is, the outer world. Fulbright, too, was a senior in the Senate, as Johnson had most notably been, and McCarthy was a junior. Johnson, expected a great deal more of Fulbright than of McCarthy.

And to cap it all, when John Kennedy was elected President in 1960, Lyndon Johnson had publicly recommended Fulbright to be Secretary of State. Musing sometimes upon all these matters, Johnson would wryly observe that he quite understood why some of the traditional allies of the United States—Belgium in particular, to which we showed the very reverse of sympathy in her postcolonial ordeals in the Congo—went about saying that the way to be well received in Washington was first to kick Washington squarely in the groin.

Perhaps most painful of all from his viewpoint, however, was the fact that the antagonists of the Vietnam policy were able to obtain a kind of copyright on the word "liberal" even when, as was most notable in the case of Fulbright, some had long records of opposition to liberal causes in this country. When, for illustration, Johnson had put through the 1957 Civil Rights Act he had appealed long and in vain for Fulbright's help. That Senator had a voting history on this issue in no substantial way dissimilar from those of such advertised archseg-regationists as Senators Strom Thurmond of South Carolina and James Eastland of Mississippi.

All this sort of thing understandably caused Johnson to feel on many days and nights in the White House that the world had been turned upside down indeed, and that the Red Queen's logic had become the philosophy of his time. Still, he never moved to the right in order to obtain from that quarter the affection or assistance that was so denied him from the left. The conservative help which came to him came in fact on its own steam. Pride was again a factor in his reticence here; perhaps more important was his instinct that if he ever accepted actual concert with the conservatives on Vietnam they might insensibly take him over.

From first to last here he had twin devils; one loudly articulate, one very quiet but in the end more dangerous to a prudent course in Vietnam. For a political section that was two-thirds simply classically conservative and one-third plainly right-wing always thought that far from doing too much militarily in Vietnam he was doing too little. Had he given these fellows their head the upshot almost certainly would have been incomparably more "escalation" in Vietnam than ever in fact occurred. If the doves were forever speaking in most undovelike tones on his left, others were forever—although far less publicly—trying to seat him upon a tiger of the right. The doves pecked him very nearly to death to be sure; but had he mounted the tiger, the country itself, to change the metaphor, might well have wound up actually, and not simply in slogan, "mired down in a land war in Asia." So he was long forced to operate between an upper stone simplistically labeled "too much" and a nether stone simplistically labeled "too little."

With his own party in embittered shambles and the opposition Republicans prepared to help succor him upon this one point but otherwise, naturally and as good partisans, ill disposed, another politician might well at least have stopped demanding costly liberal domestic programs as a gesture of reconciliation with the conservatives. But not Johnson. The time never came when he was prepared to say that Congress had done enough in the area of social reform; the time never came when he had not drawn up "just a few more bills" for that social Reconstruction which had been his central objective in happier days. So much in welfare in all its aspects was done so long and so often that even welfare's advocates tended both to lose count and, most improbably, even to lose interest. He made it all look so easy—apart from the fact that for reasons previously given there was so little substantive and analytical examination of how far he was going—that it all wound up looking infinitely less significant than it really was, whether viewed affirmatively or negatively.

When Richard Nixon succeeded to the White House, for illustration, it was so plain as to be all but universally conceded that the country needed a breathing space in order to digest the very flood of reform that had gone before. Where Johnson had run, Nixon set out sedately and slowly to walk. If the mood of the nation did not itself command this course, as it seemed to many it really did, then the simple administrative realities certainly did. For Johnson himself, though commonly considered primarily a political tactician, was in truth much abler as innovator than as implementer. Thus, again, the legend; thus, again, the reality.

He always fancied himself acutely able in the field of management; this he never was. His antipoverty program turned up obvious shortcomings in many places and sometimes undeniably gross abuses, such as paid "training" for Negro militants in the arts of fomenting public disorders. Brought to his attention, such episodes never had the degree of Presidential attention or intervention which surely they should have had. His inclination was to mutter angrily against "crackpots"—but then to pass on to the immensely compassionate and useful work that was being done for and by other Job Corps trainees and, especially, among sick and handicapped children.

And even when he muttered the word "crackpot" he uttered it without malice or real anger. For invariably he proceeded upon the assumption that crackpotism was better, at least, than hard, uncaring efficiency.

Too, he had very often been called a crackpot himself, from the right wing, and this had never bothered him. The odd truth is that, down underneath, he really rather *liked* crackpots. Though it is almost certain that he had never in his life read Dante, it is altogether certain that Dante's famous remark about weighing the sins of the warm-blooded and cold-blooded on different scales was wholly expressive of the life view of Lyndon Baines Johnson.

Thus when associates got into trouble—whether the

somewhat overadvertised troubles of Bobby Baker, Johnson's sometime staff helper in the Senate, or some other poor devil—the Johnson approach usually was the precise opposite of that of Dwight Eisenhower. Johnson's instinct was to recall the biblical admonition against casting stones. Right away, in such circumstances, he would begin to think of extenuating circumstances, of human frailties and so on. For those about him, and notably for those positioned by life below him, he felt a powerful personal accountability. He would denounce them privately and face to face at the drop of his large Texan hat; he would defend them nevertheless to the end from all "outside" danger or even criticism at almost any cost.

That all these attitudes were unsuitable to the Presidency is certainly true, but that they expressed a rather different personality from the personality so long put before the public is no less true. He had a loud bark, but it was far worse than his bite when he was dealing with those less powerful and advantaged than himself. If any Cabinet officer or other person of high rank—apart from Robert Kennedy—had ever sought to challenge him with naked impertinence, there would have been a memorable burst of Johnsonian fire. And yet there was this episode: A young secretary-typist in the President's private office had gone on leave, and when she returned she found her chair occupied by another. Someone of slightly higher rank had thought to send her off to some other Federal job, possibly with the President's absent-minded approval, more likely not. At any rate, she herself was having none of this. She marched to the Presi-

dent's own desk and cried out, "How would *you* like it
if you went off on vacation and came back to find that
Hubert Humphrey had stolen *your* chair?" Johnson, the
incomparably tough and all that, looked up at her in
momentary astonishment, found amusement overturn-
ing anger, and grumped at her, "All right, damn it, take
your blasted chair and shut up, will you?"

The word "tolerance" to him had an utterly private
connotation and no other. Mass intolerance, racial, religious or whatnot, had no place at all to him, though of
course he recognized its existence, simply because it was
literally foreign to his nature; it was irrelevant and absurd. He could be tolerant toward a person; he could not
be tolerant toward a race, a class, a grouping, because an
act of tolerance in such cases would have implied the
possibility of a substratum intolerance that had never
existed in him in the first place.

As the first President to place a Negro in the Cabinet
and a Negro upon the Supreme Court he was of course
by no means unconcerned with the possible value of
these steps in his never-ending attempts to seek liberal
approval. And yet even more deeply he saw these as acts
of reparation by the first Southerner (unless one consid-
ers the long-removed Woodrow Wilson) to hold the
Presidency since Andrew Johnson. If they helped him
politically, that was all to the good; in any case they
would help in history—and history defined as his re-
gion's no less than his own. He declined staff urgings at
the time publicly to put this cast upon the matter, but
this was simply because that was his way. An acute and
independent friend once said of him that when he did

that which was questionable he did it to the blare of every trumpet; when he did that which was good, he did it by stealth and in the dark, almost as though hoping nobody much would notice. This view was, of course, exaggerated; yet it had a large element of truth in it.

For this was one of the most complicated politicians of his age and one of the least able to fit comfortably into that general leveling-off process in the American society toward which he himself consciously contributed so much. To the right wing he was at times almost maniacally a "do-gooder"—at home, that is—and yet, somehow, most of the right wing could not humanly sustain the hostility toward him which elementary logic would have required of it. A Wall Street banker en route to the 1964 Republican National Convention which was to choose Barry Goldwater to contest Johnson almost angrily explained his personal dilemma to his seatmate in the aircraft. "Johnson," he said, "is perhaps the damnedest spender we ever had in the White House and I don't see how in hell I can vote for him come November. And yet I guess I'm going to. Don't ask me why; I suppose it is because that while, God knows, he tosses public money around, you somehow get the feeling that he still knows what a dollar *is* and that he doesn't hate my kind of fellow."

The reaction of much of the left wing to this same Johnson was even more opaquely unreal. He annoyed, and even infuriated, the ultraliberals because they somehow could not ever get a grip upon him. They were repelled by the powerful and sometimes harshly practical streak that showed in him even in his most advanced reformist designs. They saw his personality in the most melodramatic and the most grossly unfair terms—that of "a riverboat gambler," of "a boss cowhand." Even his exceptionally powerful physique put them off; his physical bigness became an affront in itself; his Texan background not simply an accident of birth but rather a direct insult. The directness and simplicity of his language in private (when his too-many White House writers were not involved) became not ordinary candor, which in fact it was, but rather "corniness," which it never really was. His easy and unselfconscious sociability (when in the mood) was turned by them into a sort of boorishness; his lack of "style" was occasion both for endless tittering and endless complaint of clear unsuitability for high office. The sensible man will say to himself, "But these unbelievably puerile things simply could not *be.*" And yet there they were.

Thus his every act became solemnly suspect and was eagerly searched for further proof that this man in the White House was an absurd and an intolerable social anomaly. When Winston Churchill died in England, for illustration, Johnson instinctively did precisely the right thing and was bitterly abused for having done the wrong thing, simply evidencing all over again that he had "no taste." To head the official American delegation of mourning to London he chose former President Dwight Eisenhower, an old wartime colleague of Churchill's, and the Chief Justice of the United States, Earl Warren. The absence from this mission of Vice-President Hubert H. Humphrey set off a great to-do among the Johnson pursuers. They did not understand the simple truth that

273

in both high protocol and American constitutional reality Warren far outranked the Vice-President: one was
head of one of the three coequal branches of the United
States Government; the other was not in fact the head of
anything.

Such episodes as this were all but countless; given a
sane atmosphere they would be far too trifling for history's least notice. But the point is that the atmosphere
was not wholly sane; the point is that the place of nasty
minutiae in the administration of Lyndon Johnson became far more effectively important than any and all of
the substantive acts of that administration. The snob-
erosion that had happened to Harry Truman in this
connection was only the smallest foreshadowing of the
snob-erosion that was to do so much to discredit Lyndon
Johnson. It was, nearly from the very beginning, an era
more suitable to psychiatric than to traditional political
analysis.

Did he make great mistakes as well as great advances?
Of course he did. But did ordinary people have much
opportunity to condemn the one and either to appreciate
or assess the other? They did not.

A half-forgotten instruction of high school English
admonished the student that language could be at once
entirely correct and wholly absurd in its effect by insen-
sitivity to priorities in importance and emphasis, as thus:
"The enemy violated the border, burned the village,
killed fifty women and children and despoiled six
chicken coops." To the most angry of his most articulate
and most enfevered critics Johnson's whole tenure had
to do, most of all, with six chicken coops. The justly

memorable and the inherently grand—whether grand in positive or negative assessment—were largely lost in preoccupied concern with the belch at the dinner table, the convertible car driven too fast, the unforgivable habit of dropping the "g." Never had so many adversaries done so much with so little—and with such little motives.

•

71 72. 73 74 75 10 9 8 7 6 5 4 3 2 1